MW00465529

FOR THE PASSERS-BY

Scribner
An Imprint of Simon & Schuster, Inc.
1230 Avenue of the Americas
New York, NY 10020

First Scribner hardcover edition November 2023

SCRIBNER and design are registered trademarks of The Gale Group, Inc.,
used under license by Simon & Schuster, Inc., the publisher of this work.

For information about special discounts for bulk purchases,
please contact Simon & Schuster Special Sales at
1-866-506-1949 or business@simonandschuster.com.

The Simon & Schuster Speakers Bureau can bring authors to your live event. For
more information or to book an event, contact the Simon & Schuster Speakers
Bureau at 1-866-248-3049 or visit our website at www.simonspeakers.com.

Interior design by Ben Prescott Design
Cover concept inspired by Bob and Roberta Smith

Manufactured in the United States of America

1 3 5 7 9 10 8 6 4 2

Library of Congress Cataloging-in-Publication Data has been applied for.

ISBN 978-1-6680-3443-9
ISBN 978-1-6680-3445-3 (ebook)

Thomas Heatherwick

Humanize

A Maker's Guide to Designing Our Cities

SCRIBNER

New York   London   Toronto   Sydney   New Delhi

PART ONE

Human and Inhuman places

PART TWO

How the cult of boring took over the world

PART THREE

How to re-humanize the world

Part One

HUMAN AND INHUMAN PLACES

Human PLACES

The best £6.99 I ever spent was on a January afternoon in Brighton in 1989, when I saw something in a student book sale that grabbed my attention.

I'd made the journey for an open day at the University of Sussex, to have a look at the Three-Dimensional Design course. Ever since I was small, I'd been fascinated by inventions and new ideas and the design of objects. Now that I was eighteen years old, I was working towards a BTEC National Diploma in Art and Design at Kingsway Princeton College in London, studying drawing, painting, sculpture, fashion, textiles and three-dimensional design. Years earlier, I'd given up on the idea of pursuing building design, because what I'd seen of that world known as 'architecture' felt cold, impenetrable and uninspiring.

But then I wandered into the student union sale, picked up this book, opened it at a random page and a switch in my brain flicked on.

There I saw photographs of a large, dirty building on the corner of a street in central Barcelona. The building was called Casa Milà; it was unlike anything I'd ever seen in my life. It simultaneously had the qualities of an incredible raw, carved stone sculpture and a contemporary apartment block.

I was stunned. I had no idea that buildings like this existed.

I had no idea that such buildings *could* exist.

If buildings could look like this, why weren't there more of them?

If buildings could look like this, what else could they look like?

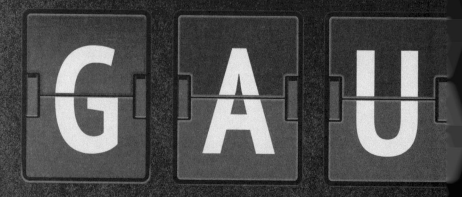

 Thirty-three years later, I travel to Barcelona
to see Casa Milà. I fly in from a meeting in
Munich and, as I queue to catch my plane, I hear one of
the passengers making a quick call. I don't speak fluent
German, and can't fully make out what she's saying.
But I can clearly understand one word – the name
of the man who made the building I'm here to see.
She keeps repeating it, every few moments: 'Gaudí . . .
Gaudí . . . Gaudí . . .'

I've seen Casa Milà in real life a number of times before this trip. But today I feel I'm able to grasp its genius much more clearly. I lead a busy studio in King's Cross, London, that's designed bridges, furniture, sculpture, Christmas cards, a car, a boat, New York City's 'Little Island' park, London's red Routemaster buses, and the cauldron in the opening ceremony of the 2012 Olympic Games. But we mainly design buildings. So I know about the forces of money, time, regulations and rules and politics, as well as all the important people who can tell you 'no' at any moment. I also understand the never-ending pressure to water down a creative vision and how incredibly hard it is to make any new building whatsoever, let alone one that is special.

I remember a recent conversation in London with a friendly architect – when I showed them that my studio and I were proposing to place a slight curve above an otherwise rectangular window, they commented, 'Wow, you're brave.' That comment was a spooky clue to me that there was something badly wrong in the world of building design. As I approach Casa Milà now, I see before me the ultimate dismissal of that scared perspective – a masterpiece by the man who apparently once said, 'The straight line belongs to men, the curved one to God.'

SLIGHT CURVE

1 4

Casa Milà is an unashamed festival of curves. The windows of its sixteen apartments look like they have been energetically carved out of a limestone cliff face. It is the opposite of flat. The front of the nine-storey building undulates amazingly in the light, dancing in space – in and out and up and down – almost as if the building itself is breathing.

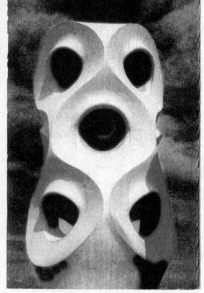

In front of the stone are balconies of wrought iron that writhe asymmetrically in abstract shapes, like giant seaweed pieces that protect you from falling. And on the roof, twisting, highly artistic chimneys and ventilation stacks sprout upwards from a large terrace. After it was completed in 1912, its critics gave Casa Milà the nickname *La Pedrera*, or 'The Quarry', because it had the appearance of having been cut out directly from the stone in the ground.

Then, as now, Gaudí's building was a sensation. The news of Casa Milà's construction was reported in popular magazines of the time such as *Ilustració Catalana*. But as celebrated as he was, even Gaudí got in trouble with the local authorities. Casa Milà broke several city building codes: it was taller than was permitted, and its pillars intruded too deeply into the pavement.

When Gaudí was told a visit by the building inspector had gone badly, he threatened that if he was forced to cut his pillars back, a plaque was to be attached, saying: 'The section of the column that is missing was cut on the orders of the City Council.' In the end the pillars were left alone, but a fine of 100,000 pesetas was demanded: a significant sum, just a little less than Gaudí's entire 105,000-peseta fee for designing the building.

As I stand on the other side of the busy crossroads, it's astonishing to think that while Gaudí and his clients were making a priceless gift to the city, the authorities were imposing a big fine on him. Even though this building was made to provide high-end apartments for wealthy people, I believe it *is* a gift. Casa Milá is an act of spectacular generosity. A selfish building cares only about its ability to make profit for its owners, and disregards everyone else. But Casa Milà reaches out to every one of us who pass it every day, wanting to fill us up with awe and break us out in smiles. Even forgetting the riches that this and other Gaudí buildings have gifted their nation as tourist attractions, the sheer joy that Casa Milà has given to hundreds of millions of everyday passers-by is unquantifiable.

Waiting at the pedestrian crossing, I reflect on what makes Casa Milà so visually successful. Partly it's a result of its gorgeously distinctive combination of repetition and complexity.

Humans seem to be drawn to repetition: I think of the columns of a Greek temple, or the repeating patterns in the timber beams of a Tudor house, or the repetitive windows in a British Georgian crescent of terraced houses. We naturally appreciate order, symmetry and patterns in artworks and objects.

But we don't like too much repetition. Just enough allows us to feel oriented and reassured; too much feels oppressively boring and tyrannical.

Humans also like complexity. As animals we're naturally curious, intelligent and easily bored. We gravitate to interesting things that invite us to look more in order to understand them. But complexity without any order or repetition can feel alarming and chaotic.

What we like is just the right combination of repetition and complexity. Not one, nor the other – but both, complementing one another. This is surely related to our evolution in natural environments. If you think of a forest of trees or ripples on a lake or the markings on a butterfly's wings, you'll be picturing a play of repetition and complexity. These are images that probably inspire feelings of quiet elation in almost everyone.

If you want to design a building that will be attractive to most human beings, repetition and complexity are vital tools. These forces can act as opposites, but they need each other. And when the balance of their aesthetic tension is right, it's possible to make works that most people will find astoundingly beautiful.

The Beatles, extract from 'Yellow Submarine'

Outside of architecture, other art forms like music and storytelling also play with repetition and complexity. The rhythm of a drum, a verse and a chorus are all patterns that can repeat in a song, but complexity is frequently then layered on top of these elements, using string instruments, lyrics, and shifts in tempo and emotional intensity. The difference between a Beatles song like 'Yellow Submarine' and a prelude by the classical composer Shostakovich is that one leans more towards repetition and the other towards complexity. They're at opposite ends of the spectrum, but they use the same essential tools. Likewise, when we read a captivating novel, or watch the latest thriller, we can sense an archetypal pattern in the story: the drama goes predictably up and down and up and down until the

Dmitri Shostakovich, extract from 'Prelude I for Piano', Op. 34

inevitable finale. We know it's going to happen, but if we're not bored, it's because the writer has added enough complexity to the ancient pattern to keep us interested.

Like a beautiful song or an absorbing novel, Casa Milà has a predictable pattern: horizontal floors, vertical columns, a grid of windows, curves of limestone. But it's also incredibly complex. It's simply not possible to understand Casa Milà at a glance, as you can with so many modern buildings. It demands that you give it a second look – and then a third and then a fourth, and then you're craning your neck and squinting at it, grinning, trying to take it all in. It feels like a joyous three-dimensional puzzle that your brain is trying to solve.

As I cross the road and walk towards the building, I note its size is perfect too. If the same windows and balconies were repeated one floor higher, or were stretched and replicated further along the street, it would become too repetitive, and the balance and magic would crumble.

As I step onto the pavement immediately in front of Casa Milà, I see the craftsmanship that's embedded into every part of it. The early part of my career was spent understanding how to make things, so I know what it's like to create objects by carving wood, chiselling stone and hammering big bits of hot steel. The ironwork on the balconies is mind-bendingly contorted and free-flowing, and from my own experience of beating iron on an anvil I can imagine the impossibility of trying to heat it and twist it and hammer it, let alone lift it. And as I look up, I can see that the ironwork is even doing something different on each of the balconies. There it is again: repetition and complexity, captured and immortalised in iron.

The stone face of the building has craftsmanship visible on its surface too. Even though it looks smooth from a distance, its creators didn't spend lots of extra money polishing away the chisel marks to make it smooth up close.

Instead it is unapologetically raw, and the tiny randomised chipping marks add yet another layer of complexity that reminds us that this is the work of human hands. It's not embarrassed to be raw and hacked. The way the light catches each one of those thousands of violent human-made notches changes with the weather and the arc of the sun, so the surface never looks the same from

What I cherish most about Casa Milà is that it is so three-dimensional; the opposite of all the flat two-dimensional modern buildings we've got used to experiencing. Standing by it at street level, it flexes in and out over the pavement. With its beautifully gradual transitions between areas of light and shadow, it feels spookily as if – just by looking at it – I am touching its surface.

Thirty-three years after I saw it in a book that still sits – tatty and flapping with Post-its – on a shelf in my studio, Casa Milà has been cleaned of the soot that coated it when I first visited. It looks better than ever. Part of what excited me all that time ago was that this wasn't an ancient castle or a royal palace from a distant era. This was a modern building that had been built for the age of the machine. It had lifts that carried its residents between floors and a back entrance that led to an underground car park. It showed me it was possible for modern buildings to be as beautiful and interesting as any work of art.

As a young man, on seeing that picture of Casa Milà, what I fell in love with wasn't one building, but the potential of all buildings. Before that day in Brighton, I'd always seen the built world as fixed. Old buildings were almost always fascinating, but new ones were almost always mysteriously dull and monotonous. Buildings looked like what they looked like and that was just how things were. But Casa Milà opened up a crack in that fixed reality.

Through that crack I caught a glimpse of the world as it might be.

See p. 494 for captions.

After a twenty-minute walk north-east of Casa Milà,
I see Gaudí's most famous building, the Basílica de la
Sagrada Família, which also embodies repetition and
complexity, but manifested to a degree that's staggering.
Built in a style that encompasses both Gothic and Art
Nouveau, La Sagrada Família has the recognisable
patterns of a Christian cathedral, but these old patterns
are melted and multiplied and entangled and decorated
in ways that mesmerise your gaze and send pops and
sparks through the brain.

Here is a building in which complexity is winning: it's
impossible to grasp it with a single passing look – or even
a dozen. The streets and parks that surround it are filled
with tourists who are frozen in their tracks. Standing and
staring upwards, they are trying to work out the thrillingly
elaborate visual puzzle. It's so complex that I would never
be able to memorise exactly what I'm looking at. It's as
if I'm staring into something infinite. The building plays

with my emotions. The first thing
I feel is awe at the bulk and the
height and the repetition of
the textured towers. And sheer
astonishment that little humans
can conceive of something like this,
and then coordinate themselves

to turn materials into it. Then, mixing in with the awe, is joy. La Sagrada Família feels like a wild celebration, not just of Gaudí's Catholic God, but also of our human capacity to achieve incredible things. *This is what we're capable of*, it seems to be declaring. *We are amazing.*
As I look closer, the building shows me its humour and gutsiness: at the top of thin spires are brightly coloured fruits – apples, grapes and oranges; Christian words of praise like *sanctus* and *hosanna excelsis* are written into its towers in great gaudy letters; real bits of wine bottles are embedded into its walls like the leftovers of a party.

Here I am, one of thousands of visitors on a chilly Thursday lunchtime in March, being completely entertained by a building that's not even finished. Gaudí began work on this project in 1883; and its estimated completion is 2026, the centenary of his death. I wonder if the young woman I overheard at the airport in Germany is in the crowd somewhere, waiting patiently to get inside.

La Sagrada Família is as extravagant and generous as buildings have ever got. About 4.5 million people join the queues to enter the basilica every year; on top of that, another 20 million people come just to look at it from the outside. This is mass-market cultural entertainment, and it succeeds by engaging and playing with human emotions as expertly as any hit song, bestselling novel or even blockbuster film.

It's a deeply human building because it connects with people and adds something to their lives. It's been created by makers who care deeply about the needs, practices and pleasures of ordinary people. You can also tell it's a brilliantly human building by the sheer number and diversity of us humans who come from all over the world just to look at it.

Afterwards I follow the trail of tourists to Barcelona's Gothic Quarter. Gaudí's Sagrada Família and Casa Milà are singular and special, whereas this part of the city is made up of hundreds of buildings that have been constructed over the space of 2,000 years. But the buildings of this place also act as mass-market entertainment, as they too attract humans by the millions. It is clearly a human place.

Why? Like Casa Milà and La Sagrada Família, the buildings of the Gothic Quarter play with order and complexity, and not just in their decorative elements such as the gargoyles and intricate mouldings above windows and doors. The unpredictable positioning of windows, the shifting heights of doors, the lumps and bumps on walls from historical craftsmen, and the undulating cobbled streets all add complexity. So do the many injuries from use over the centuries: scratches and patches from accidents and repairs; worn paved walkways, smoothed by the soles of millions of feet. There's complexity in the materials of wood and unpolished stone and shabby brick; there's complexity in all the ways that centuries of weather have marked and eroded the surfaces in organic shapes and patterns; there's complexity in a set of iron studs on a door, each one of which is surrounded by a halo of dirt where centuries of cleaning cloths haven't quite made contact with the oak underneath.

Nothing is truly flat in the Gothic Quarter. There's three-dimensionality everywhere you look, even in the alleyways that change

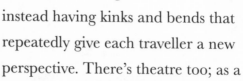

in width and never travel for long in a straight line, instead having kinks and bends that repeatedly give each traveller a new perspective. There's theatre too; as a tall, mysterious passageway full of shadows opens out suddenly and dramatically onto a surprisingly sunny cobbled square that has an orange tree planted just off-centre, I realise that if I'd approached the same square from a wide, straight street, it wouldn't have been anywhere near as exciting. I feel like an adventurer making a series of fantastic discoveries.

There are also hints or fragments of stories everywhere I look. Just like the words and symbols embedded in La Sagrada Família, which speak of Christian lives and myths, there are shrines on corners and worn carvings that would have once drawn attention to long-lost businesses, with the strange shields of ancient guilds and societies.

It's sometimes said that we look at our buildings to find out who we are. In the Gothic Quarter, the identities of generations of Catalans certainly speak out confidently from its thousand surfaces.

This place gets its humanness not from being designed by a lone genius such as Gaudí,

but by having been built – bit by bit, year by year – by hundreds of designers who are now mostly unknown, and who had a habit of giving people not only what they needed, but also what they wanted. It's functional and would be regarded by a majority of people as beautiful. What makes the work of Gaudí so brilliant is that he managed to learn from the human-engaging qualities and features of buildings such as these, and then reinvented them into something new, without directly copying any individual detail.

And he did it to the same joyfully human-attracting result.

To me, whether it's the streets of the Gothic Quarter or Gaudí's buildings, these are palaces that have been built for ordinary people. They feel like a celebration of humanity – of human needs, wants and actions. Nobody needs to pay a penny to experience them. They are uplifting and inviting and offer much more than the minimum. These buildings remind me of the subway stations in Moscow and Stockholm that give travellers theatrical experiences every time they go anywhere. While not being so obviously 'buildings', they too offer

Moscow

more than the minimum, and succeed in entertaining thousands of people every day with their generous human qualities.

Like the buildings of Gaudí and the Gothic Quarter, these subway stations were built with human wants, needs and actions in mind. They were also created with the expectation that they could be loved by the many, and last far beyond the lifetimes of their makers. They were not built simply to make money for a landlord, or to be the headquarters of an insurance company for thirty years before being demolished. They were made to last for hundreds of years.

Nobody sane would allow such widely loved structures to be needlessly demolished.

The only thing that could cause their destruction would be natural disaster or war.

37

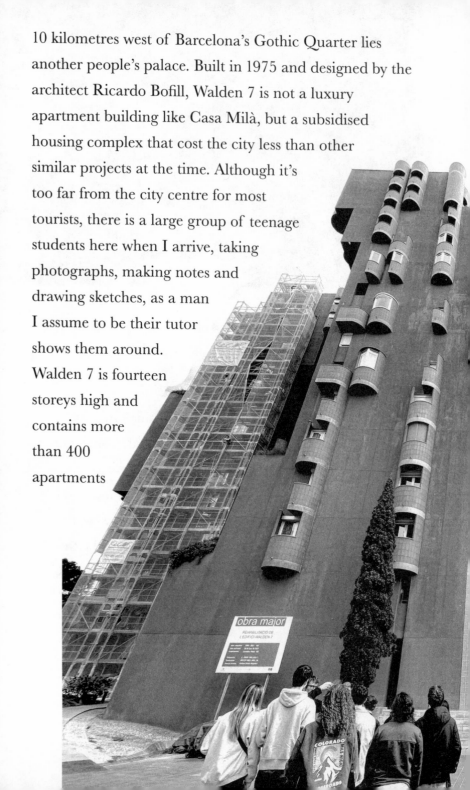

10 kilometres west of Barcelona's Gothic Quarter lies another people's palace. Built in 1975 and designed by the architect Ricardo Bofill, Walden 7 is not a luxury apartment building like Casa Milà, but a subsidised housing complex that cost the city less than other similar projects at the time. Although it's too far from the city centre for most tourists, there is a large group of teenage students here when I arrive, taking photographs, making notes and drawing sketches, as a man I assume to be their tutor shows them around. Walden 7 is fourteen storeys high and contains more than 400 apartments

in eighteen towers that are clustered around five courtyards. Like those designed by Gaudí, it's a generous building, and works hard to inspire emotions of awe and fascination – and not just in the people who live there. Coloured a deep terracotta red, with an unusual locally appropriate Moorish sense of place, it's impossible to grasp Walden 7 with a quick look. Its windows emerge from cylindrical balconies that are arrayed in complex patterns over its surface. Its walls are also three-dimensional and unpredictable, shifting in and out every few floors. This is a building that makes you stop in wonder. The entrance to Walden 7 isn't mean and small, as you might expect from an 'affordable' housing project. Instead, it is deep and grand and pierced dramatically by shadows and shimmering blue tiles. Walking inside, it feels like entering an alien palace from a work of science fiction.

It's a fundamental part of human nature that we all need to believe we're special, no matter who we are or where we come from. Walden 7 was built as social housing for people lower on the socio-economic ladder, and every day, as they come and go, they experience a building that wants them to feel like superheroes. This isn't an expensive structure made from expensive materials for expensive people. And yet huge amounts of care and attention have been poured into its design, and that sense of care and the pride that follows will have buoyed its inhabitants for decades.

As I stand on a low wall, watching the students' tutor pointing at the roof, I have the same thought as I did thirty-three years ago at that book sale in Brighton.

If some buildings can look like this and make me feel this way, why aren't there more of them?

Two weeks later, I travel to Vancouver in Canada and stay at a hotel close to the waterfront. Across the road is a big plaza that stretches to the edge of Vancouver Harbour that's wide, mostly flat and virtually empty of people. There's lots of visible repetition, but very little complexity. Along the side of the space are some tilting lamp posts and the yellow awnings of the Cactus Club Cafe. A large sculpture that was the Olympic Cauldron of the 2010 Winter Games has been placed at its entrance, translucent rods resting on each other in a kind of tent shape.

Apart from the sculpture, there's nothing much to nourish your brain in the buildings that surround you. Thank goodness for the choppy grey water in the bay, the snow-capped mountains in the distance, and a buzzing seaplane circling in to land in the harbour.

On the city side of the plaza is a forest of towers constructed from steel and glass. They're uniform in look and all roughly the same colour – silvery aluminium with panes of green glass. There's something thin and impermanent and empty about these towers, and also completely anonymous. They could be anywhere in the world: on the Equator or near the Arctic Circle or in Singapore or Anchorage or Nairobi or Perth.

In amongst the faceless towers, I see a <u>single interesting</u> ✳ <u>roof.</u> The building it belongs to is made of brown brick and grey stone; sections of varying heights cluster up towards its centre, and it has a greenish pyramid on its top. It appears complex – I have to look at it a few times to figure it out.

I head towards it, crossing between cars and walking up concrete stairways. In front of the buildings I pass, I see more sculptures. Their purpose seems to be to distract passers-by from all the anonymous structures that have been thrown up around them. They feel like apologies – confessions of failure for uninteresting new buildings. In fact, I know this is true. When I first started my studio and dreamed of being commissioned to design whole,

real buildings, we were instead repeatedly commissioned to make objects that were designed as artworks, just like these. Such objects masqueraded as artistic expressions, but in reality were pieces of design for disillusioned clients who had realised their places wouldn't be interesting enough without them. These artworks were there to compensate for the otherwise-poor public experience caused by weak building design.

I soon find myself on the other side of the road from the structure with the interesting, clustered roofs – the Marine Building. Naturally, and without thinking, I study the ground floor for a moment, then lean backwards, my gaze travelling rapidly up the structure's height, until it reaches the top, where it settles for another moment, taking in the details of the roof. This is how most of us instinctively take in tall buildings. The makers of this one – architects McCarter & Nairne – seemed to understand this. Its most interesting elements are at the bottom and the top, the same places the eyes automatically want to rest. And its most energetic elements are concentrated in its first 40 feet, where the greatest number of people experience most buildings.

VANCOUVER HARBOUR

Completed in 1930, eighteen years after Casa Milà, the Marine Building is a skyscraper made in the Art Deco style that was fashionable at the time. It isn't curvy, like the works of Gaudí, but it doesn't need to be. It's quite complex, it's quite repetitive, and although much of it is plain, inexpensive brick, it's also selectively lavish and generous. Its walls have sufficient human touches only where it really matters. As I cross the road towards it, I begin to make out images on its surface: fish, seahorses, lobsters, starfish, crabs, Zeppelins, submarines, ocean liners, battleships, steamships, famous explorers' ships – Francis Drake's *Golden Hind*, Captain Cook's *Resolution* and Vancouver's own HMS *Discovery*.

Like Walden 7, the Marine Building has an entranceway that makes its inhabitants and visitors feel special. Two wide revolving doors are framed with gold, and a rising sun throws out great shining beams over a wooden-hulled ship with billowing sails and a crucifix at their centre. High on top of the sun fly six huge Canada geese. Almost every surface in the parts closest to people on the ground has complexity either carved into it by hand or present in the natural appearance of its material.

There's so much to take in that, just like in Barcelona, I have to stop for a while and allow myself the enjoyment of trying to understand its riddle. When challenged about the actual function of the Marine Building's so-called extravagant touches, the architect John Y. McCarter defended them by saying he wanted to create 'something that appeals. Now you know as well as I do, you try to get that, but you don't always get it . . . The old Vancouver Hotel had something, you see? It's the atmosphere, they tried to get it in the new hotel, but they never did. You haven't got anything there, but the old hotel – it had atmosphere.'

I've never seen the old Vancouver Hotel (or indeed the new), but it seems to me that McCarter did achieve his aim of giving his building 'atmosphere'. It has an aura to it, as well as its own personality.

It triggers a delicate cascade of emotions. It entertains. It's generous in spirit. It tells a story about adventure and discovery and the wonders of the sea. It reminds us that the world around us is interesting and alive.

It feels like the work of human beings who care deeply about human wants and human needs.

Leaving the Marine Building, I walk deeper into the city. The wide, straight thoroughfare of West Hastings Street offers nothing of the mystery and adventure of Barcelona's Gothic Quarter. It isn't just the street's width that's the problem. Rather, this doesn't feel like a human place. It feels like it was built for the inhuman interests of cars and money.

To my right is the Pinnacle Hotel Harbourfront. Unlike the hefty but layered Marine Building, and the tall narrow structures of the Gothic Quarter, it feels ostentatiously horizontal, like a skyscraper that's been tipped onto its side. As humans walk through a landscape with their heads tilted around ten degrees downwards, they're primed to look along and in front of themselves, rather than up and down. Too much emphasis on long horizontal lines tends to create an oppressively repetitive effect. The only cure for that horizontal repetitive monotony is complexity.

But there is none of that here. Walking past the Pinnacle Hotel Harbourfront I see mostly large panes of glass and plastic signage. Its huge windows go all the way from the ceiling to the floor. This is a common feature of modern shops, cafes and offices that's supposed to maximise light and commercial display-space, but in reality it just

IS THE BOTTOM OF THIS BUILDING
INTERESTING TO WALK PAST? ⟶

focuses the human gaze on people's bags leaning against the glass, wastepaper bins, and scuffs where vacuum cleaners have hit table legs and walls.

Above the flat dark windows and a red sign is a horizontal wall of pale concrete. Because a decision was made not to have any of the roofing overhanging the front of this wall that could channel the rainwater away from it, years of dripping water has stained its surface with ugly vertical streaks.

STAINED AND UNLOVED

DOES ANYONE CARE ABOUT THIS UFO ON TOP?

Unlike the buildings in Barcelona, which are full of interesting lumps and bumps that help them hide dirt and the signs of ageing in an unusual way, these unadorned surfaces act as a blank canvas for highlighting decades of pouring and staining rain.

Above the concrete strip is a featureless black horizontal wall over which grow a few bedraggled, misshapen shrubs. And above these are the high walls of hotel rooms arranged in blank, repetitive grids. There's no playful complexity in the design and, as a result,

you can understand the entire thing with a single passing glance. Weirdly, the most interesting features are the stains. There's also a strange UFO-like disc at the top, overhanging the roof of the building, which is probably a restaurant. But this wasn't made for passers-by, who are unable to see it very well from the street.

Where is the 'atmosphere' that John Y. McCarter once spoke of? Where is the entertainment? Where are the stories? Where is the celebration? Where is the generosity? Where is the feeling of care? Where are the human touches? If you are going to put a huge building on a busy street for thousands of people to experience every day, shouldn't you be interested in how to make people in the surrounding area feel good, and not just your hotel guests in the insides of their rooms?

On the next block, I pass a thin wall of ivy barely covering a large array of air-conditioning outlets, pushing hot dirty air into my face as I walk. Whatever this building is, it's obviously decided that this is its backside, not its front, so it doesn't matter how it appears or how it behaves. It doesn't seem to care that this is a major street in a world-renowned city that many thousands of people travel through every day. After having experienced generosity in the buildings of Barcelona and elsewhere in Vancouver, here is an encounter with selfishness.

Why, in the prosperous twenty-first century, are we surrounded by structures like the Pinnacle Hotel Harbourfront and not more buildings like Walden 7?

Constructions like Walden 7 show us that it is possible, in modern times, to make human buildings that don't cost prohibitive amounts of money.

So why don't we do it?

Why do we keep on making buildings like this?

If you're not in the building business yourself, you might be surprised by the answer.

Sometime in the early decades of the twentieth century, as the Marine Building and Casa Milà were being constructed, there was an astonishing revolution in the way we thought about buildings. A radical new set of ideas about how they should look swept through academic and professional circles, and then took over the world.

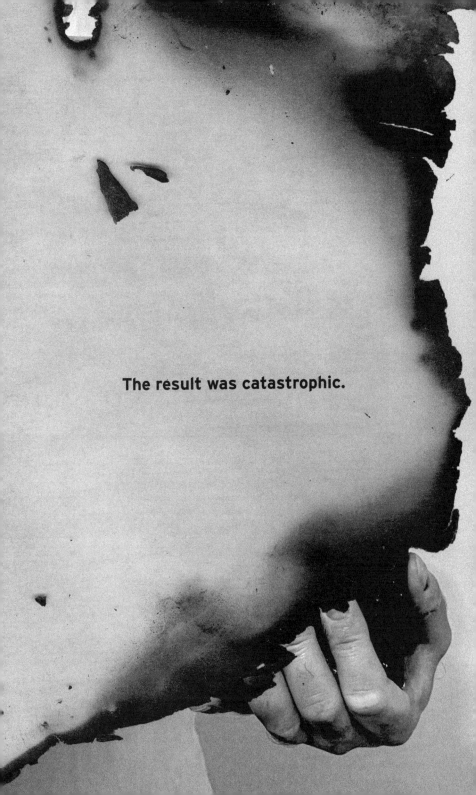

5 013922 061948 >
Item Number: 6194
Datei Kasten
Boîte de Rangement
Archivo de Caja
Box Bestand

GREECE

ARGENTINA

Russia

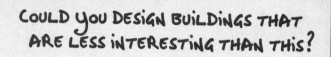

COULD YOU DESIGN BUILDINGS THAT ARE LESS INTERESTING THAN THIS?

BRAZIL

Why did a city say yes to so many of these?

ITALY

Would you go on a date outside these buildings?

WOULD THE PERSON WHO DESIGNED THESE BUILDINGS WANT TO LIVE IN THEM?

How generous are these buildings?

Kenya

INDIA

IF YOU ASKED CHILDREN TO DRAW AN IMAGINARY DREAM CITY, HOW MANY WOULD COME UP WITH SOMETHING LIKE THIS?

HOW MANY SECONDS WOULD IT TAKE TO MEMORISE THE DESIGN OF THESE BUILDINGS?

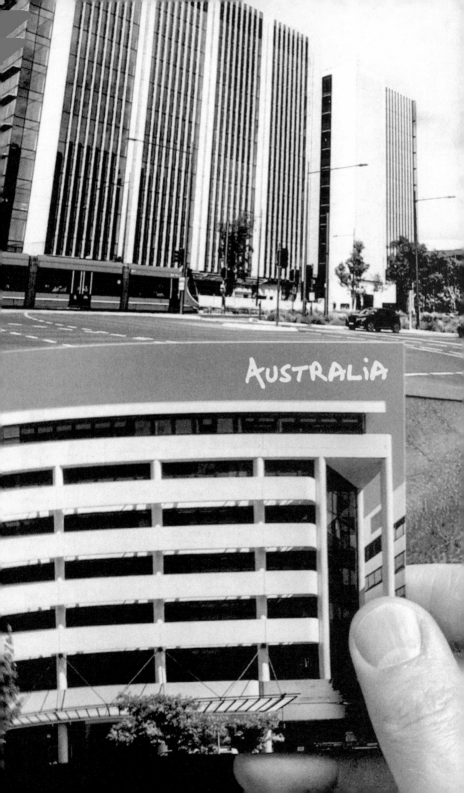

JAPAN

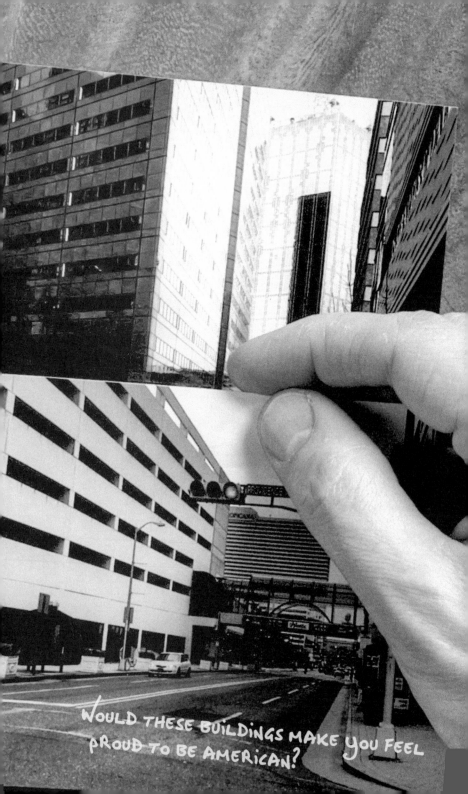

WOULD THESE BUILDINGS MAKE YOU FEEL
PROUD TO BE AMERICAN?

THE ANATOMY
OF A CATASTROPHE

Before we discover how this global epidemic of inhuman buildings spread through the world, I should explain why it matters.

I want to talk about the importance of the outsides of buildings rather than the insides. This isn't because I believe the insides don't matter. They matter a lot, but they only matter to the people who go inside the buildings. Also, it's relatively easy to change how the interiors of buildings feel, with paint and objects and furniture. The outsides of buildings are different. They matter to everyone who goes past them. And that's a lot more people. But most of us are truly powerless to change how these outsides make us feel.

For every individual person that spends time inside an office or block of flats, there will be hundreds or even thousands of people that pass by the outside of that building every day.

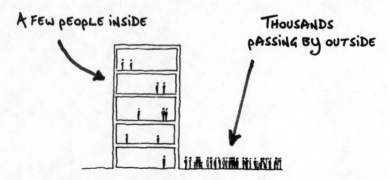

A FEW PEOPLE INSIDE

THOUSANDS PASSING BY OUTSIDE

Just like at Casa Milà and the Pinnacle Hotel Harbourfront, the outside of that building will affect every single one of those people. It will contribute to how they feel.

As they walk down the street, and they pass by dozens of buildings, they'll feel dozens of emotions.

And those emotions add up.

Those emotions matter.

They matter more than we realise.

Over the last hundred years or so, the outsides of the ordinary buildings we pass by every day have taken on a certain 'look'. You know the look I mean: we saw it in Vancouver, and in the pages you've just flicked through. It's present in towns and cities all over the world.

This look has turned out to be astonishingly harmful. The places that have been built for us, that have adopted this look, make us stressed, sick, lonely and scared. They've contributed to division, war and the climate crisis.

This look we stumbled upon a century ago has been a global catastrophe.

There's a word that describes the kinds of buildings
I'm talking about.

I don't like this word. It's bland, vague and forgettable.
It seems unserious.

This word doesn't do justice to the harm it describes.
It fails to capture the intense and dreadful changes that
have been creeping through our towns and cities for the
last 100 years, bringing with them destruction, misery,
alienation, sickness and violence.

I wish there was a better word I could use – one that,
when you heard it, gave you a truly visceral sense of what
I'm convinced is a century-long global catastrophe we're
still in the grip of.

But when I think about this catastrophe, and I think
about these buildings, I always come back to this word.

So here it is.

BORING.

I did warn you.

When you hear the word 'boring', you almost certainly think: 'A whole book about the boringness of buildings . . . *really?* We have so many problems in the world: social injustice, the climate crisis, political polarisation, war, tyranny and corruption. And you're making a big song and dance about . . . *boring buildings*?!'

And then you might quite reasonably think: 'Who the hell are you to call something boring anyway? Just because *you* don't like this shopping centre or that office block, it doesn't necessarily mean it's bad.'

If you are thinking these things – well, I don't blame you. If I were you, I'd probably be thinking them too. I can only ask you to hold on, for just a few more pages.

There are some serious issues to consider that affect billions of people.

By the end of this part of the book, I hope to have convinced you that we're under attack from a plague of boringness, and that it really is a global catastrophe.

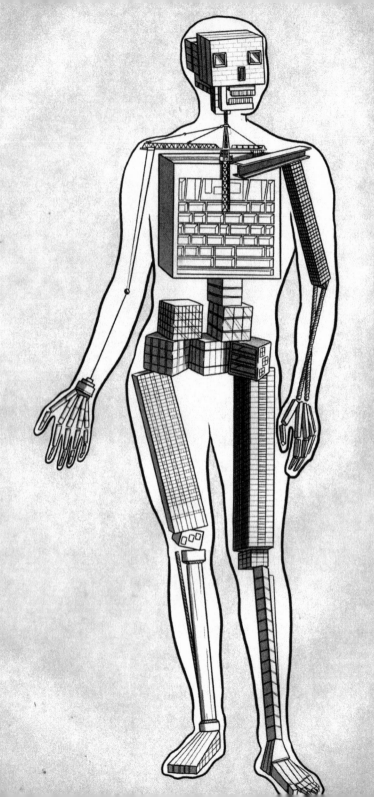

THE ANATOMY OF BORING

What does boring
actually mean?

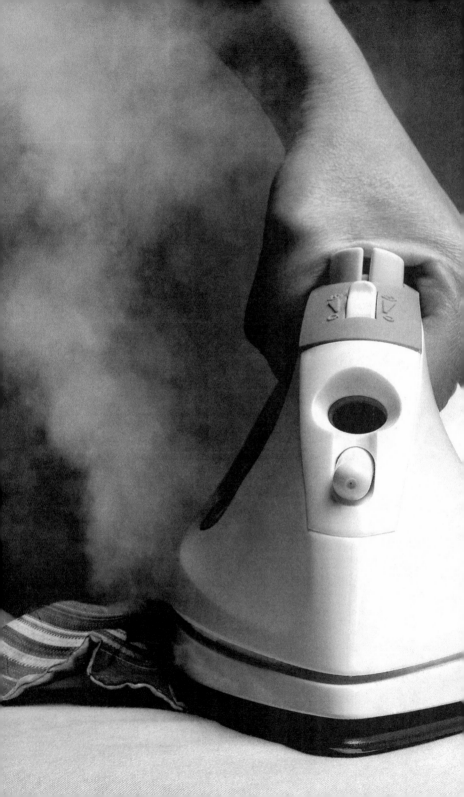

The fronts of modern buildings tend to be incredibly flat.

Their windows and doors barely stick in or out.

Their roofs are often flat too.

The lumps and bumps in buildings matter because they create interest. As we saw at Casa Milà, depth creates interest either by sticking out and breaking up straight lines, or by creating surfaces that light and shadows can play on. In countless subtle and intricate ways, a building with depth changes its appearance with the movements of the sun – a patch of brightness here, a nook of darkness there – the light flowing in and out of doorways and window frames as the Earth turns through the day.

When buildings are too flat, they are punishingly boring.

TOO PLAIN

Modern buildings lack ornamentation.

When you look at buildings that were constructed more than a century ago, it's striking how much care their designers took to add flourishes of complexity.

These buildings have patterns, details and decorations.

They have lumps and bumps and crevasses and curls and crenellations and cornices and points that stick up and out and in and around. Even everyday buildings that weren't thought of as 'special' or 'important' were made with this mindset – with an interest in interestingness and what was thought of as beauty at the time.

**When buildings are too plain,
they are boring.**

TOO STRAIGHT

Modern building design tends to be based on rectangles. There's nothing inherently wrong with this approach (classical buildings were the same), and it makes a kind of logical sense because it's highly practical. It's also much easier to design things with straight lines and right angles – even more so with the latest building design software that most easily draws squarish shapes.

But the exclusive use of straight lines and rectangular geometry has got wildly out of hand. When used on buildings at scale and in the absence of any other kind of shape, they tend to create scenes of repetitive horizontality, and feel hard and utterly unfriendly to walk past. They are inhospitable to human beings. Given that there are virtually no straight lines or right angles in nature, they are also astonishingly unnatural.

Remember the architect who, on hearing I wanted to put a slight curve on the top of a rectangular window, called me 'brave'.

What's so scary about a curve?

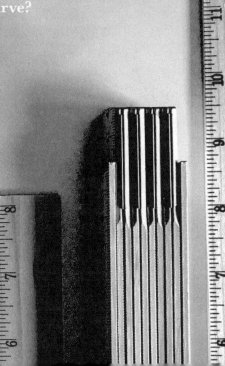

TOO SHINY

The outsides of modern buildings tend to be made from smooth, flat materials such as metal and glass. Shiny materials can be lovely, but when entire buildings – and even entire districts – are made from only hard-feeling reflective materials, our senses become numb with indifference. This lack of variety has a profoundly desensitising effect.

New buildings often have large pieces of relatively thin glass clipped together in place of solid walls with windows. Even when they also have large areas of metal panelling, the surfaces of all of those materials still tend to be uniformly smooth and flat, which provides nothing for our senses to latch on to.

The most extreme example of this is the construction industry's invention of curtain wall glazing – by which the entire outsides of buildings can be made of nothing but huge sheets of glass. When this is used, any human interest and variety that the outsides of buildings could have is virtually killed.

When buildings are too shiny, they are boring.

The increase in glass on buildings has also
contributed to mass bird slaughter.
It's been estimated that, in the US alone,
between 100 million and 1 billion birds die every
single year as a result of flying into windows.

TOO MONOTONOUS

Modern buildings often take the form of rectangles that are made up of smaller rectangles. These rectangles are arranged in a grid.

If a straight street is lined with these grid-like buildings, the landscape becomes a repetitive queue of large, flat, shiny, plain rectangles.

These buildings look monotonous from a distance.

And they look monotonous from up close.

This kind of monotony doesn't inspire or excite or fascinate human beings.

The places in which we're forced to live and work end up looking a bit like this: monononononononon onononononononononononononononononononononononon onononononononononononononononononononononononon onononononononotony.

TOO ANONYMOUS

More than 100 years ago, the outsides of buildings tended to capture something of their place; they were, in some sense, articulate. They told a story about where they were, and who they were for. Today, they mostly don't.

This 100-year catastrophe has been a cultural revolution. It's ruthlessly stripped new buildings of their personality and sense of place.

When buildings are too anonymous, they are boring.

WHAT DOES THIS RECENT BUILDING SAY ABOUT THE ORGANISATION INSIDE IT?

TOO SERIOUS

When you look at these kinds of office buildings,
what do you feel?

You feel serious, perhaps even a little intimidated. These
are serious buildings for serious people, in which serious
lives are being lived. Why do buildings need to look
serious? Why were their creators so scared of making

somewhere that makes people feel joyful? These sorts of buildings are only capable of evoking one kind of feeling. They suffer from an extreme case of emotional austerity.

When buildings are too serious, they are boring.

WHEN IS BORING NOT BORING?

But, having said all that, it's important not to
become fixated on every one of these points.

Sometimes,
flatness is charming.

Sometimes,
plainness is elegant.

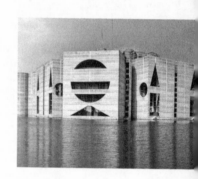

Sometimes, straight lines are exciting.

Sometimes,
shininess makes you smile.

Sometimes,
monotony is entrancing.

Sometimes,
anonymity is necessary.

Sometimes, serious
is just right.

See p. 494 for captions.

WHEN IS BORING BORING?

In the right contexts, and with the right intentions, the base elements of boring can be wonderful. But when too many of these elements come together in one building or one place, boringness becomes a serious problem.

The way I see it, boring is like an equation.

It's like putting too much sugar, fat, carbohydrate, alcohol and nicotine into a human body. More often than not, it's the combination and accumulation over a lifetime that kills you.

When too much boring happens
in one space, it becomes . . .

harmful boring.

How can boring be harmful? Isn't boring an absence, a pause, a piece of nothing? Nothing can't harm you. Nothing is nothing, after all.

But the astonishing and little-known truth is that boring is worse than nothing.

A lot worse.

Boring is a state of psychological deprivation. Just as the body will suffer when it's deprived of food, the brain begins to suffer when it's deprived of sensory information.

Boredom is the starvation of the mind.

A neuroscientist called Colin Ellard has studied how this happens. In 2012, he travelled to New York City to analyse how people felt when they walked through a boring place and then, shortly afterwards, through an interesting place. He wanted to know: how would spending just a brief amount of time in these different places affect a person's mood?

This was the boring place. It's the outside of Whole Foods, a large supermarket on New York's Lower East Side. It takes up an entire block.

This is an interesting place in the neighbourhood, similar to the one Ellard chose. It's just a short walk away from Whole Foods.

As the groups walked through each location, a specially designed smartphone app asked them questions about what they were seeing and how they were feeling. Outside the supermarket, the most common responses included *bland*, *monotonous* and *passionless*. However, down the block from Whole Foods, the most common responses included *socialising*, *busy* and *lively*.

But the truth is Ellard didn't need an app to identify how their moods were being altered. It was obvious. 'In front of the blank façade, people were quiet, stooped and passive,' he wrote in his account of the study. 'At the livelier site, they were animated and chatty, and we had some difficulty reining in their enthusiasm.' One rule of the study stipulated that participants shouldn't talk to each other. At the Whole Foods Market, maintaining silence wasn't a problem. But at the interesting location, the researchers lost control of their subjects. The rule of silence 'quickly went by the wayside. Many expressed a desire to leave the tour and simply join in the fun of the place.'

Ellard was also collecting data on the participants' emotional states from special bracelets that took regular readings from their skin. These bracelets were detecting a state that scientists call 'autonomic arousal'.

Autonomic arousal refers to how alert we are, and how primed we are to respond to threat. It's a measure of stress.

When Ellard checked the results, he discovered that people in the boring location weren't simply feeling nothing. Their autonomic arousal – their stress levels – had gone up.

The boredom wasn't just making them feel nothing. Their brains and bodies were going into a state of stress.

You can imagine why being chased by a predator or being locked up in prison might start to stress you out. But why would a boring *place* make you stressed?

Scientists have found that when we enter any environment, we unconsciously scan it for information. During the millions of years in which our brains were being moulded by evolution, we lived in nature. And natural environments are crammed with complexity. Every single second, our senses deliver around 11 million pieces of information about our environment and surroundings to our brain. The human brain has evolved to expect this base level of information, a bit like the body expects base levels of oxygen, water and food.

Boring modern landscapes, which privilege repetition over complexity, supply us with an unnaturally low level of information. Ellard theorises that walking through them is a bit like having a phone conversation, but you're only hearing words like 'it' and 'so' and 'the'. There's *some* information there, but it's repetitious, non-complex and of extremely low quality.

When the brain is deprived of information from its environment, it takes it as a signal that something is wrong. It panics. It switches the body to a state of alert, raising its readiness to deal with danger.

More than 100 years ago, it would have been extremely hard to find a truly boring external urban environment. Today, boring environments are everywhere. We're blanketed in boringness.

If simply walking through a boring landscape is stressful, what happens when we're forced to live our entire lives, year after year, in boring homes? What happens when we're forced to work our entire careers in boring offices, boring factories, boring warehouses, boring hospitals and boring schools?

When we're bored, our stress hormone – cortisol – spikes. When cortisol levels are too high for too long, we become more susceptible to a variety of terrible illnesses, including cancer, diabetes, stroke and heart disease. One major scientific survey in the UK found that 'those who report being bored are more likely to die younger than those who are not bored'.

Boringness has also been found to be an accelerator of a nasty range of negative behaviours. Reporting by *Scientific American* finds that boredom generates a higher risk of 'depression, anxiety, drug addiction, alcoholism, compulsive gambling, eating disorders, hostility, anger, poor social skills, bad grades and low work performance'. Researchers at King's College London found that, in studies, boredom generates 'greater risk-taking across financial, ethical, recreational, and health or safety domains'. Episodes of boredom are one of the most common predictors of relapse in addicts. Scientists have even found an excess of boredom makes it more likely that people will adopt extreme political beliefs.

Humans are not well suited to a life of boredom.

Boring buildings make us malfunction.

Boring buildings are inhuman.

Modern urban places that are flat, straight, plain, monotonous, anonymous and serious change how we feel and how we behave. These Kingdoms of Boring make us antisocial.

Housing built more than 100 years ago tended to be relatively low-rise, rarely more than seven storeys high. Even properties that were shared by people with extremely low incomes usually had features such as backyards, front yards and broad front steps. These buildings typically faced each other, and were lined up along a street.

Backyards, front yards, broad front steps and streets are all places that encourage humans to look, linger and chat. In places where humans look, linger and chat, there is more likely to be a sense of community.

When we live in low-rise housing, or along well-designed terraced streets, we're primed to gradually make acquaintances. These acquaintances might begin as the briefest nods of acknowledgement as we encounter each other in backyards and front yards, and on front steps, pavements and streets

Those nods can turn into smiles.

Which can turn into recognition.

Which can turn into small talk.

Which can turn into bigger talk.

Which can even turn into friendships and life-enhancing relationships that help make our lives more meaningful.

This is how the design of the outsides of buildings can have a profound effect on our lives and the shape of our societies. At their best, they tip us towards each other, increasing our chances of positively connecting with one another. Humans are social animals. We tend to suffer when we don't feel securely connected within a supportive network of people, and we thrive when we do.

In the twentieth century, we threw away the idea of the street with terraced housing and replaced it with separated housing blocks surrounded by open spaces and lacking all the ground-floor social details. In 2008, scientists in the US looked at the effects that different kinds of buildings had on elderly people living in the poor Hispanic neighbourhood of East Little Havana in Miami, Florida. They found that simply being without 'positive front entrance features', such as porches or broad entrance steps, led residents to be nearly three times more likely to suffer from health problems. Although some of this difference was thought to be related to the direct physical benefits of climbing steps to porches, also important was the fact that those who lacked these semi-social spaces at the front of their housing had weaker ties to their community and were therefore more socially isolated.

To be human is to be social.

When we're socially isolated, we become sick and sad, and we die sooner.

Boring places make us antisocial.

Boring places are inhuman.

← NEIGHBOURS CELEBRATING VE DAY, LONDON, 1945

For years, scientists have been gathering a powerful mass of evidence that shows people are happier and healthier when in the presence of nature.

Dr Frances E. Kuo of the Landscape and Human Health Lab at the University of Illinois has studied these effects in The Robert Taylor Homes, a notorious housing project in Chicago. When it was built in 1962 it was the world's largest public housing complex, comprising twenty-eight sixteen-storey concrete towers. The development was also violent and dangerous. How did the residents cope with the strains of living in such a place?

Kuo realised that some apartments at the Robert Taylor Homes looked out onto 'green' courtyards planted with grass, shrubs and trees. Others looked out onto courtyards that were concrete and grey. Aside from this the apartments were identical: of the same design, and inhabited by people of a similar background and socio-economic status. Could something as simple as a view of a tree make a difference?

This gave Kuo an opportunity. She began knocking on doors and talking to women who lived in the project – some around the green courtyards and others around the plain, grey ones – gathering information on aspects of their mental well-being. When she took her data back to the lab, she found something astonishing: the green courtyarders were less stressed, more focused, and were better able to deal with life's difficulties than their unlucky neighbours who overlooked the grey courtyards. They also saw their personal problems as less severe, less long-standing, and more likely to be solved at some point in the future.

In poor inner-city neighbourhoods, Kuo concluded, the simple act of 'planting a few trees may help provide individuals and families the psychological resources needed to "take arms against a sea of troubles"'.

How can this be?

Humans evolved in nature. We feel better in nature. Twenty seconds in nature reduces our heart rate. Five minutes in nature brings down our blood pressure. Incredibly, a simple view of trees from a hospital window has been shown to help patients recover from surgery faster – so much so that they were released, on average, a full day sooner than if they had views of brick walls. They were also found to experience less pain (as measured by their consumption of painkillers) and were judged by their nurses as being more emotionally resilient.

More recent research, by academics at the University of Warwick, has added a fascinating new twist to what's now well understood about the power of nature. They wanted to find out precisely what kinds of environments actually made people feel good.

They analysed more than 1.5 million ratings of 'scenic-ness' of 212,000 images of places in Britain. They then compared these ratings to how happy and healthy the actual residents of these places reported themselves to be. Just as the researchers expected, people reported themselves to be happier and healthier in surroundings that had more scenicness. But here was the twist: it turned out that scenicness didn't necessarily mean 'natural'. Happiness and health also increased in urban places that were considered scenic.

One of the researchers, Dr Chanuki Seresinhe, wrote that 'the old adage "natural is beautiful" seems to be incomplete: while nature features such as coastlines, mountains and canals can improve the beauty of a scene,

OXFORD – ITS BUILDINGS ADD TO ITS SCENIC BEAUTY

flat and uninteresting green spaces are not considered beautiful. Interestingly, characterful buildings and stunning architectural features can improve the beauty of a scene.'

Researchers like Seresinhe have now moved on from the argument that what humans need to thrive is mere greenery.

What they actually need is scenicness.

Which sounds like another vague and useless word. But further research has uncovered what adds to an urban place's scenicness. A survey of people's views of 19,000 streets and squares in London, Manchester, Birmingham, Milton Keynes, Canterbury and Cambridge found people most enjoy places that:

Do not look like they've been 'designed by committee'.

Have a strong sense of place and 'could not be anywhere'.

Have 'active' façades that 'live' and show a variety of patterns.

That are, to put it another way . . . not boring.

ARE THESE SCENES MORE SCENIC WITH

Canaletto, *Eton College*, 1754

John Constable, *Salisbury Cathedral from the Meadows*, 1831

OR WITHOUT THE BUILDINGS?

(WOULD SOMEONE HAVE BOTHERED TO PAINT
THESE WITHOUT THE BUILDINGS?)

BORING PLACES CONTRIBUTE TO DIVISION AND WAR

Marwa al-Sabouni is an architect from Homs in Syria. She has investigated how places that were built in her city over the last 100 years helped stoke the civil war that engulfed her country.

The original, ancient heart of Homs was a realm of porches, steps and twisting alleyways, with many drinking fountains and benches in the shade of fruit trees. The design of the buildings and streets encouraged people to move slowly, pause and chat with one another.

'A brief chance encounter in the street would be the occasion for the fastest "download" process between one person and another,' al-Sabouni writes. 'They would exchange news, family history and any other updates in the blink of an eye, then equally resume their paths.' Homs was a city in which Christians and Muslims 'lived, worked and worshipped together'. Churches and mosques were built side by side; the ringing of bells accompanied the call to prayer. Followers of these faiths 'shared everything – house walls, shops, alleys; even a church/mosque'.

Then came a new style of building and street that formed new kinds of neighbourhoods: 'inhumane architecture . . . brutal, unfinished concrete blocks, neglect, aesthetic devastation, divisive urbanism that zoned communities by class, creed or affluence'.

These new neighbourhoods separated people – 'Sunnis, Alawites, Shiites and Christians of all creeds; villagers and Bedouins' – into groups. And these separated groups lived separate lives in boring, serious, anonymous buildings that 'enhanced social stagnation and introversion, since they created no shared identity or attachment to a place'.

Unlike in the old city of Homs, where different groups shared distinctive spaces and characterful buildings and became familiar and relaxed with one another, these dull new places encouraged insular thinking, as tribe was separated from tribe, and religion was separated from religion. Instead of the citizens feeling as if they all belonged to the city of Homs, as they once had, the people felt they belonged only to their own group. 'The common experience of the city was lost; any sense of belonging dissolved at the boundaries of inward-looking groups.'

Eventually, perhaps inevitably, 'the urban segregation turned into sectarian conflict'.

Of course, Homs wasn't flattened and hundreds of thousands of people killed simply because the populations were separated by new zones and alienated by new architecture. But al-Sabouni is convinced the 'modernisation' of the neighbourhoods is one reason among many that helped cause the conflict. And she doesn't want you to be fooled into thinking this kind of slide into conflict couldn't happen in the West. 'When I read about heterogeneous urbanism in other parts of the world involving ethnic neighbourhoods in British cities or around Paris or Brussels,' she says, 'I recognise the beginning of the kind of instability we have witnessed so disastrously here in Syria.'

Boringness: ruining lives for 100 years and counting. And arguably playing a part in the loss of hundreds of thousands of lives.

PEOPLE DON'T LIKE BORING PLACES

When over 2,000 Americans were asked to rate pairs of images of public buildings – one traditional-looking, the other modern – they consistently rejected the modern option. This was true no matter which section of the public was asked. No matter their age, race, gender or socio-economic background, they preferred the traditional-looking buildings by a margin of nearly three to one.

The same has been found in my own country. An analysis of a series of surveys of the British public's taste in architecture concluded that 'somewhere between 15 and 20 per cent of the population are likely to have some sympathy for mainstream modern architecture'. A dislike of mainstream modern architecture turns out to be one of the few things that unite Britons as a people. In 2021, the think tank Policy Exchange ran a survey in conjunction with Deltapoll, asking the public to rank ten images of local government buildings according to how much they liked the 'look, style, design and beauty'. The rankings – in which modern styles sat at the bottom – were 'fundamentally similar across different demographics'. The favourite, the Neo-Georgian Bristol City Hall, found itself placed at the top, 'regardless of age group, gender, region, economic group and voting intention'. It might be tempting to conclude from all this that people simply prefer buildings that look old. But this isn't true.

BRITAIN'S TEN
MOST LOVED BUILDINGS

A 2015 survey found two of Britain's most-loved buildings were built in the last 100 years. And unlike most modern buildings, those two are not boring.

The Shard

The Houses of Parliament

Stonehenge

The Eden Project

Buckingham Palace

Edinburgh Castle

Westminster Abbey

St Paul's Cathedral

Windsor Castle

Blackpool Tower

THE WORLD'S TEN MOST LOVED BUILDINGS

Global studies find the same thing. The world's top
ten buildings, as measured by the most popular Google
searches, include seven that were built within the last ✳
100 years. It's not new buildings that people hate.
It's buildings that are boring.

Empire State Building

Notre Dame Cathedral

Taj Mahal

The Shard

Gardens by the Bay

Burj Khalifa

Eiffel Tower

Hallgrímskirkja

Musée du Louvre

La Sagrada Família (still being built)

ENVIRONMENTAL

BORING BUILDINGS HELP TO CAUSE CLIMATE CHANGE

But then so do interesting buildings.

There's no getting away from it: commercially available concrete and steel are terrible for the environment, no matter what kind of structure they find themselves a part of.

A total of 11 per cent of annual global carbon emissions comes just from construction and building materials. That is five times the amount of carbon emissions as the entire aviation industry.

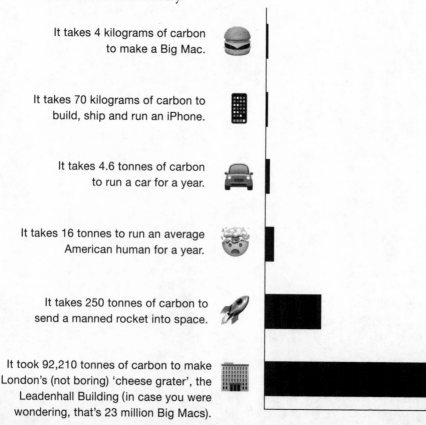

It takes 4 kilograms of carbon to make a Big Mac.

It takes 70 kilograms of carbon to build, ship and run an iPhone.

It takes 4.6 tonnes of carbon to run a car for a year.

It takes 16 tonnes to run an average American human for a year.

It takes 250 tonnes of carbon to send a manned rocket into space.

It took 92,210 tonnes of carbon to make London's (not boring) 'cheese grater', the Leadenhall Building (in case you were wondering, that's 23 million Big Macs).

So, once we've spent the carbon costs necessary to put a building up, it's crucial that it stays there, being useful, for as long as humanly possible. <u>The worst thing we can do is knock that building down after just a few decades</u>, and <u>put something new up.</u>

This is why boring buildings are much worse for the environment than interesting ones. They're much worse because, as we've discovered, they're unpopular. Over the last 100 years a disastrously high number of unloved developments around the world have been torn down and replaced – often with newer but no less boring buildings.

They're also more likely to require demolition because they've started falling to bits. The boring styles that took over the world in the twentieth century had 'shorter cycles of repair and higher rates of obsolescence', according to a 2013 report published by the Getty Conservation Institute. 'Modern buildings exhibit myriad physical problems, many arising from the nature of their external [walls].' Many of these buildings begin to show 'signs of obsolescence after only twenty or thirty years in service'. Twentieth-century buildings have mostly not been designed to look good when they're old.

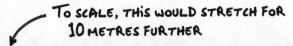

To scale, this would stretch for 10 metres further

The reality is that shiny-smooth buildings are not usually maintained like shiny-smooth cars in showrooms – they become neglected and are cared for only sporadically. Unless they've been designed with materials and a complexity of design that can look good dirty and that will work with this lack of love, they always end up looking shabby.

The editor of *Architects' Journal* has called demolition 'construction's dirty secret'. Every twelve months, around 1 billion square feet of buildings in the US are demolished and replaced. This is equivalent to half of Washington DC being knocked down and rebuilt every single year. In the UK, 50,000 buildings are knocked down annually, generating 126 million tonnes of waste, and the average

commercial building has a lifespan of around forty years. Incredibly, almost two-thirds of all the waste generated by the entire country is produced by the construction industry.

In China, 3.2 billion tonnes of waste were produced by the construction industry in 2021, the vast majority of it from demolition. That figure is estimated to rise to more than 4 billion tonnes by 2026.

If building a building is bad for the environment, then building a building, knocking it down, and building a new building where that building once stood is much worse.

Boring buildings are unsustainable.

BORINGNESS IS A
SOCIAL JUSTICE EMERGENCY

Our most vulnerable people live in
the most boring buildings. Why should absence
of boredom be a luxury good?

THE BURNT-OUT FRAME OF GRENFELL TOWER
SOCIAL HOUSING, LONDON, 2017

SO THIS IS
WHAT WE KNOW:

Boring places make us stressed.

Boring places make us sick.

Boring places make us lonely.

Boring places make us scared.

Boring places contribute to division and conflict.

Boring places are unsustainable.

Boring places are unpopular.

Boring places are unfair.

The Strange Fact of Prize-Winning Boring

Some industry professionals love to tell each other that the work they're doing is visionary. They give themselves awards. They say their buildings are 'poetic' and 'timeless' and 'innovative' and 'eloquent' and have 'integrity' and 'vision' and 'honesty' and 'mastery' and 'clarity' and 'lightness' and show 'a deep commitment to the art of space' and 'an unyielding commitment to place and its narrative' and make 'significant contributions to humanity'.

When it's pointed out that most people don't actually like boring buildings, they reject those concerns as ill-informed, silly or backward-looking. They and their supporters accuse their critics of 'plain ignorance or visual blindness' and of being reactionary, conservative and anti-progressive – sometimes even going so far as to smear them by associating them with the far right.

Some architects see themselves as artists. The problem is, the rest of us are forced to live with this 'art'. It's not possible to avoid it, like we can avoid a boring film or a boring novel or a boring painting. Their 'art' becomes the places in which we're all forced to live, work, shop, heal and teach. Their 'art' becomes the boring streets we walk down every day – the streets that make us feel stressed and unhappy and lonely and which degrade our lives and weaken our communities and poison our planet.

As you read these words, there are professionals in studios drawing flat, plain, shiny, anonymous, serious rectangles and squares, and declaring them to be elegant, honest, visionary and stunning.

Concrete is being poured.

Cranes are lifting huge flat panes of glass into place.

Boring buildings are going up in towns and cities all across the globe.

Currently, more than half of the Earth's population lives in an urban area. By 2050 that number is expected to rise to over 70 per cent.

A world of harmful boring is being built for us to live in, whether we like it or not.

PART TWO

How the Cult of Boring Took Over the World

W H A T

is

an

Architect

?

The Pantheon in Rome is one of the most interesting buildings I've ever encountered. Built 2,000 years ago, it has the largest unreinforced concrete dome on the planet. Its creators were so ambitious that, two millennia later, not only is their building still loved and standing, its roof remains a world record holder. But the roof isn't the only thing that astonishes me about the Pantheon. I remember looking in amazement at the huge 7.5-metre-high bronze front doors that still open and close perfectly in their frame with a precision that is phenomenal. Even if I wanted to, it's difficult to imagine that I could order doors with that kind of tolerance today. Hardly any modern manufacturer could make them.

LINCOLN CATHEDRAL

I often have a similar thought when I'm wandering past
medieval cathedrals. Hardly anybody would have a clue
how to make a building with that kind of complexity
today. How did we modern makers of buildings become
so unambitious and unimaginative? Yet, with all our
new materials and machines and computer technology,

WESTMINSTER ABBEY

how do we allow ourselves to simultaneously still believe
we're somehow smarter than the builders of the past?
It makes me wonder if our modern arrogance masks
a sense of defeat. Are we secretly scared that we're not
as good anymore?

And it's not just the temples and cathedrals. Before the twentieth century, even ordinary and humble buildings had a level of interest that we've lost.

Here's a Mudhif meeting house in Iraq. Its design dates back 5,000 years.

Here are some nineteenth-century 'beehive houses' in Turkey based on 3,000-year-old designs.

Here's a nineteenth-century Māori meeting house
in New Zealand.

Here's a seventeenth-century almshouse in Malmesbury,
England. It incorporates a twelfth-century doorway.

Some of these buildings might appeal to your personal sense of what's attractive, and some might not.

THIS ROOF IS MADE FROM SEAWEED

Perhaps you think one is too ostentatious,
another too primitive and another profoundly ugly.
I might agree with you.

But I'd also argue that none of them are boring. Even those buildings in the past that were constructed by ordinary people on a modest scale had details, patterns and three-dimensionality. They often had decoration

and a sense of place. The culture of the builders and the inhabitants were built directly into them. For thousands of years all over the world, most of the buildings we built were interesting.

M. VITRUVII POLLIONIS
De
ARCHITECTVRA
LIBRI DECEM.

AMSTELODAMI,
Apud Ludovicum Elzevirium.
ANNO cIↃ IↃC XLIX.

12/4

Around the time that the Pantheon was being built, a Roman master builder and engineer called Vitruvius published what's thought to be the first book ever written on the subject of making buildings. In *de Architectura* (opposite) he wrote that buildings should have a combination of *firmitas*, *utilitas* and *venustas*.

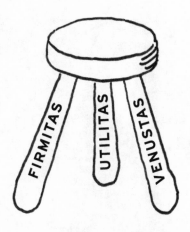

The first word means 'strength'. It shouldn't fall down.

The second word means 'utility'. It must usefully serve the purpose for which it was built.

The third word refers to Venus, the Roman goddess who was the embodiment of beauty. Vitruvius was saying the final essential quality of buildings is that they should give joy.

These three words were like the three essential legs of a stool.

Buildings designed to look good and
trigger positive emotions were usually
(perhaps even always) interesting.

They had depth, ornamentation,
patterns, details and often some curves.
They also tended to exhibit a unique

sense of place. In the days before most
people could read, religious stories
were built into buildings in the form
of sculptures, mosaics and stained-
glass windows. We used interestingness as a way of communicating

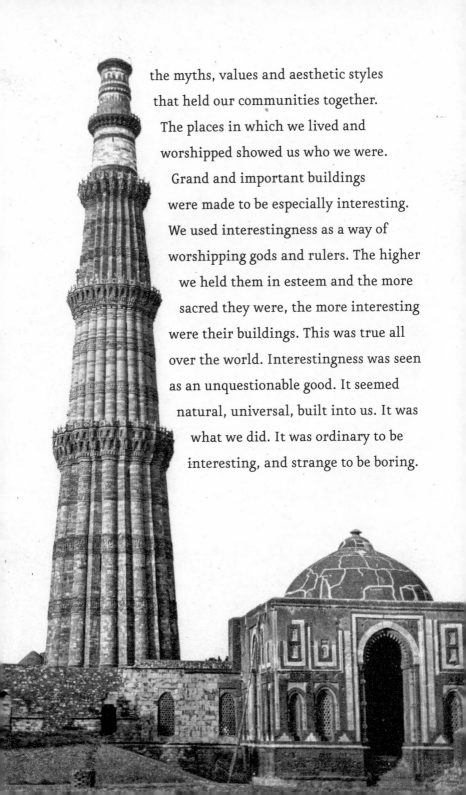

the myths, values and aesthetic styles
that held our communities together.
The places in which we lived and
worshipped showed us who we were.
Grand and important buildings
were made to be especially interesting.
We used interestingness as a way of
worshipping gods and rulers. The higher
we held them in esteem and the more
sacred they were, the more interesting
were their buildings. This was true all
over the world. Interestingness was seen
as an unquestionable good. It seemed
natural, universal, built into us. It was
what we did. It was ordinary to be
interesting, and strange to be boring.

When I look at the buildings on these and on the preceding pages I get a powerful sense of interestingness as something that comes naturally to our species. Since the beginning of time, the buildings we made looked and felt human.

But then, in the twentieth century, that changed.

A strange new way of building arrived that was quite unlike any that had existed before in the history of the world.

Boring buildings began to be erected all over the planet – in Europe, the US, South America, Asia, Africa, Australia and the Soviet Union.

All of a sudden and with astonishing speed, boringness took over the world.

THE ARCHITECT

Before I can tell the story of how strange and harmful boring-ness colonised the world of architecture, an important question must be addressed.

What is an architect anyway? This might seem like a silly question. What's an architect? What is architecture? Isn't it obvious?

Here's the answer I assumed to be true when I was a young man: architects design and make buildings.

But this is not correct.

The story of what an architect is (and is not) actually has a long and surprising history, which stretches back hundreds of years. Up until the sixteenth century, construction projects in Britain were designed and managed not by architects but by craftsmen

known as 'master builders'. These master builders left many of the smaller decisions as to how their buildings looked to other craftsmen they worked with. Many individual, talented and creative makers were given the job of ensuring their own corner of a building project had strength, utility and beauty.

This started to change in the late sixteenth century, when complex new styles from Renaissance Europe became fashionable. The master builder and the craftsmen who worked with them – the makers – were unfamiliar with these new designs and the special techniques required to construct them. The makers began to lose their influence over the look of the buildings they built.

This was the beginning of a dangerous divide in the business of building buildings that continues to this day. A new kind of person came into being: an individual who understood these grand new Renaissance ideas.

The architect.

The architect wasn't a maker. It was the architect's job to draw up a building's plans and supervise its construction by the makers, who now found themselves demoted to just doing the architect's bidding.

At first, architects still had to undergo the same training in craftsmanship as the makers. But this requirement began to fade. In 1550, the Italian painter and architect Giorgio Vasari reflected old-school thinking when he wrote that:

'Architecture can only attain perfection in the hands of those who possess the highest judgement and good design, and who have had great experience in painting, sculpture and woodcarving'

By the end of that century this view seemed outdated.

The famous British architect Inigo Jones, whose work in London in the first half of the 1600s included the layout of Covent Garden, the Banqueting House in Whitehall and the Queen's House in Greenwich, wasn't a craftsman by background but rather a draughtsman and costume designer.

By the beginning of the nineteenth century, architects had completely separated themselves from the makers. In the US, self-taught architect (and future president) Thomas Jefferson was designing major buildings such as his house, Monticello, after teaching himself from books written by Renaissance masters – especially his idol, Andrea Palladio. Architects now weren't craftsmen by background. Instead they handed down their instructions to builders through sets of complex drawings over which they had a monopoly. The Royal Institute of British Architects was established in 1834, and it officially defined the architect as separate from the makers. In 1890 it became obligatory for all architects in Britain to register with the Institute. It was now illegal to call yourself an architect unless the Institute approved of you.

The dangerous divide had been completed and formalised. The seeds of future catastrophe were sown. Architects were not makers of buildings anymore. They had become white-collar intellectuals, elevated and validated by the British monarchy yet disconnected from the creative process of making. Meanwhile, the artisans and craftspeople who actually made everything were relegated, and were seen as blue-collar workers who had no right to a creative voice in the realisation of buildings.

It was the year after my chance encounter with Gaudí in the Brighton bookshop that I discovered the extent of the gulf between architects and the process of making buildings.

I'd been lucky to grow up around makers. My mother designed and made jewellery and would take me to different craft fairs and

workshops, where I would be fascinated watching people welding, forging, casting, blowing glass, knotting, weaving and carving with all kinds of different materials. My grandfather was a writer and a music teacher. His wife, my grandmother, was a textile designer who studied at the Berlin equivalent of the Bauhaus in the early 1930s. She dressed like an elderly ballerina and had worked

for an architect called Ernö Goldfinger, who designed the Trellick Tower in London.

My grandmother had a huge influence on me. She was both modern and unrelenting in her pursuit of excellence. She spoke often about beauty, a word she'd noticed people seemed scared to use. I spent many inspiring hours with her.

As a child I dreamed of becoming an inventor and builder of special and beautiful things. Making and fixing were normal for me. I was eleven when I learned that the thing I wanted to be had a name, and it was called a 'designer'. My father and I were in the West End of London, and a few minutes down the road from

Piccadilly Circus we saw a wide-open door with a bright sign above it saying 'The Design Centre'. Inside were electronic knitting machines, robotic arms that used hydraulic fluid instead of electricity, gorgeous products and pieces of furniture, and at the centre of it all a huge spotlit model of a new incredible-looking city called 'Milton Keynes'. It was as if a kind of homing instinct switched on in my brain. I suddenly had a sense of purpose and direction.

171

On leaving school I did a BTEC diploma in General Art and Design at Kingsway Princeton College in London. After that I joined a degree course in Three-Dimensional Design at Manchester Polytechnic where I designed and made many kinds of different objects and experimented with everything that the tools, materials and equipment could do. As I began the second year I was invited to a special architecture Winter School in Edinburgh where a selection of world-famous architects gave speeches about their work. In between lectures I'd mix with the architecture students trying to make conversation.

> 'Have you ever mixed concrete?'
> 'Have you ever done wood joinery?'
> 'Have you ever laid bricks?'
> 'Have you ever welded?'

Or,

> 'on your summer holiday have you ever worked on a building site?'

The answers were always the same: 'No'. The students were as perplexed by my questions as I was by their answers. It was bizarre. None of them seemed at all interested in actually making things. On my course at college I'd been working with wood, metal, ceramics, glass and plastics – the main materials that buildings are made from. I'd learned how the process of practically

experimenting and playing with these materials wasn't a menial task but actually gave you ideas. I'd stood at a folding machine and knew what folding metal was like. I'd seen injection moulding and laser cutting. I'd carved

wood. I'd shaped wet clay with my hands

and then watched it dry. I'd chipped plastic with a chisel and sharpened the chisel in my hand.

I'd blown glass and wanted to touch it but knew I couldn't because even though it looked cold it would burn my skin off. I was by no means the best welder, the best carver, the best joiner or the best glass-blower but I'd learned to do all those things. I'd found that when you played with materials they became your teacher and showed you everything they could and could not do.

173

Making could be both infuriating and inspiring, but it was one of the best triggers for my imagination. When I looked around me at the world of objects, whether at a small silver ring or a gigantic bridge, I did so with the mind of a maker. When I worked on my own projects, I had all the theories and philosophies in my head of why design could be one way or another, but I also had a gut sense of how materials and processes affected each other and could help make better things. It was not just drawing in my sketch-book that helped me have ideas; making taught me what was possible, and making inspired me to push as hard as I could against those limits.

And yet the world-famous architects and their students I met in Edinburgh weren't at all interested in making. Their creative ideas didn't seem to have anything to do with the amazingness of what materials could do. Instead, it was largely intellectual. A place of jargony words that normal people never used, and theory that my teenage instincts told me was putting the emphasis in the wrong place. I also had the strange realisation that the famous architects everyone was listening to in awe had barely built anything real. This seemed particularly absurd. How could you be a famous architect if you'd built virtually nothing?

And how could you be responsible for making the largest objects in the world and be uninterested in making and materials?

But perhaps I'd got the wrong impression. Maybe my experience didn't represent what was really going on.

After another year of studying and getting more and more interested in the design of buildings, I decided to use the writing of my obligatory 12,000-word dissertation to research exactly what relationship designers of buildings had with making. I spent the summer of 1991 working on 'The Inspiration of Construction: A Case for Practical Making Experience in Architecture' – driving around the country talking to builders, joiners, teachers and fourteen architects. I filled my little black and burgundy Citroën 2CV Charleston car with watermelons as thank-you gifts for the people I met.

But I discovered my experience at the Winter School was by no means an exception. The general attitude was summed up by a lecturer at the Architectural Association, who told me: 'You don't need to be able to saw a piece of wood to know whether you prefer a smooth door.'

So there it was. The gap that had begun opening up in the sixteenth century between the makers and the architects had grown wider than ever.

I'd once assumed architects to be people who designed and made buildings.

But I'd discovered that architects aren't makers. So that must mean they're designers?

But that isn't quite right. Architects don't always see themselves as designers, either.

I first got an inkling of this as a young teenager. As I'd become increasingly interested in design, my parents would take me to exhibitions and shows. When I went through a car design phase, my father bought tickets for the London Motorfair at Earl's Court. I was fascinated by the futuristic designs for vehicles I saw that day. Then, as I became interested in the design of buildings, my father took me to the Architectural Association on Bedford

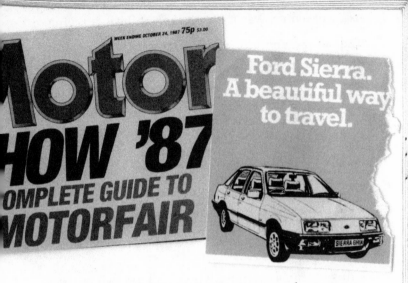

Square to see the degree show, where students were exhibiting their work. I was excited. As far as I understood it, architects designed buildings and buildings were the biggest objects it was possible to design. It was design on the largest canvas imaginable. It would be exciting to see the work of the building designers of the future.

What I saw that day left me baffled and disappointed. At the car show we'd seen visionary designs of futuristic cars. But at the architecture show there were no apparent designs of buildings. There were no discernible walls, roofs or windows. Instead there were a series of inexplicably complicated abstract drawings on the walls, and long bits of writing containing ideas I couldn't comprehend, about such things as the 'multi-layered complexity of the politics of spatial programming'.

177

As I worked my way through the exhibition, trying to understand anything at all, a metal machine in the middle of the floor made twitching movements with clanking metal arms.

It made no sense. I'd been expecting to be awed by sublime visions of the future. Instead I was looking at visual gibberish and tripping over a twitching machine. The work of these young architects seemed impenetrable. What was going on?

Things became clearer a few years later, when I was a twenty-one-year-old design student at Manchester Polytechnic. For our degree shows we needed to design and make our final pieces. Some students made earrings, some made wooden plates and others made benches. Inspired by my experiences with Gaudí and a trip to Barcelona the previous year, as well as everything I'd discovered while writing my dissertation that summer, I decided I wanted to try to make a real building. I knew this was ambitious. I also knew that students on the architecture course never built anything. Even my own tutors were quick to say, 'Why don't you make a model of your building instead?' But given my dissertation research, I felt somehow provoked to want to try. Also, I knew the Victorians had a tradition of building small structures in the form of pavilions, follies and gazebos. Maybe a modest structure like one of those might be achievable?

One weekend, when I'd been exploring the countryside around Berwick-upon-Tweed in Northumberland with my girlfriend, I'd seen a strange derelict barn whose roof had slumped and twisted. It made me wonder what would happen if you carried on twisting the roof all the way to the ground, so it wasn't just a roof but also a wall. And if I did that on both sides, could I turn that idea into a small pavilion?

Back at college, I was excited by the potential of doing something like this. I went to see the senior tutor in the architecture department. Surely they would love the fact that a college student was going to create a full-size building and would want to help with me with it if they could. I sat enthusiastically at the tutor's desk and showed him the initial drawings and clay models of the design, and then waited quietly as he studied them. Eventually he looked up and said, 'What's the poetry of your idea?' 'Oh,' I said stiltedly. 'Well, you see the roof is twisted and this is —' 'This . . . ?' he said, handing back my drawings. 'This is not architecture.'

CLAY MODEL

The leader of the architecture course couldn't muster any interest or excitement about my attempt to design and make a building. I felt sad and astonished. It seemed ridiculous to say that my design was 'not architecture'.

This was my first lesson in how the official world of building designers saw itself. The word 'architecture' was not a  description of an activity, but a prize to be bestowed. In the end I managed to find sponsorship from twenty-six generous local companies who helped me to make my pavilion in the central courtyard of the polytechnic, surrounded by the windows of various departments.

As fellow students and college technicians saw me getting soaked by the Manchester rain, they also took pity on me and helped me get it built, somehow inspired by this unusual thing that was happening.

But weirdly, when the time came for the degree shows, the architecture department blocked their windows with black paper so visitors to the show wouldn't see that a student from another department had made the college's first real building.

If an architect is a designer of buildings and I'd designed a building, then why wasn't the building I'd designed architecture? Why did it require 'poetry' to count?

Because, as I'd first sensed at the Architectural Association on Bedford Square, architects don't see themselves as just designers.

'Architecture is art,
nothing else'
Philip Johnson, architect

'Architecture is a visual art,
and the buildings speak
for themselves'

Julia Morgan, architect

'I want to specifically
talk about architecture
as an art. That's the
only reason it's
worthwhile, I believe'

Paul Rudolph, architect

'Architecture is the greatest
of the arts'

RICHARD MEIER, ARCHITECT

'The mother art is architecture'
Frank Lloyd Wright, architect

Architects see themselves as artists.

To be clear, this is a generalisation. Some of them don't. But many do. And even those who say they don't often think, speak and behave as if they do. (Recall the sorts of things they say about each other's buildings when they're awarding prizes.)

Just like other artists such as painters, novelists and musicians, architects have been vulnerable to being swept up in the artistic fads and fashions of their time. This is how the boring buildings we've been looking at and describing in these pages originally came to be. Their qualities of boringness aren't simply the result of cost-saving, laziness or lack of imagination. They didn't become boring by accident or mistake. Their boringness is on purpose. It's the result of a craze in the arts that began over 100 years ago.

That craze was called . . .

MODERNISM.

Modernism was an artistic response to the birth pangs of the world we know today.

IN THE LATE **19TH** AND EARLY **20TH** CENTURIES, almost everything we thought we knew about reality began to seem as if it was wrong.

The First World War had left a generation in a state of shock and disillusionment.

Industrialisation was spreading over the world, and inventions like

>THE MACHINE GUN
>
>THE CINEMA
>
>THE CAR
>
>THE TELEGRAPH AND
>
>THE AEROPLANE

were redefining the apparent limits of nature.

Old attitudes towards class, religion and gender were beginning to crumble. New theories about the unconscious mind that swirled beneath the fragile veneer of the 'RATIONAL' mind became popular.

Advances in science, such as Albert Einstein's theory of relativity, began to reveal the secrets of the universe itself.

The world was being shown to be more <u>DISTURBING</u> and <u>UNPREDICTABLE</u> than anybody had previously imagined.

Suddenly, the assumptions of the past seemed naive, deluded and false.

THE MODERNISTS'

creative brains, understandably and unsurprisingly, wanted to represent this challenging new reality. The art they made reflected a general '<u>LOSS OF FAITH IN REALITY</u>', writes the expert in Modernist literature Professor Pericles Lewis. 'The Modernists had to invent brand-new means of representation for the modern world.'

The old rules of painting, sculpture, literature, poetry, music and dance felt inadequate and even quaint. They were thrown out. Music became atonal, poets abandoned meter and verse structure, and authors like James Joyce dispensed with the traditional form and plot of the novel.

Pablo Picasso, *Bust of a Seated Woman*, 1960

Painters were no longer interested in pastoral scenes of windmills, topless maidens or ships in the sea. Now they wanted to strip away unnecessary detail and uncover forms that were more fundamental. They worked with pure geometric shapes, simple lines, block colours and abstract patterns, while Pablo Picasso depicted women using two-dimensional, reorganised, deconstructed forms. Objects in art galleries were no longer just trying to trigger emotional pleasure in viewers. They were trying to challenge them. The pioneering poet Charles Baudelaire wrote that the Modernists sought to 'shock the middle classes'. The artist Kazimir Malevich exhibited a painting of a single black square, whilst Marcel Duchamp exhibited a urinal, a snow shovel and a copy of the *Mona Lisa* on which he'd drawn a moustache and the letters L.H.O.O.Q., meaning *Elle a chaud au cul* or 'She is hot in the arse'.

L.H.O.O.Q.

Marcel Duchamp, *L.H.O.O.Q.*, 1919

The art of the Modernists was maddening, demanding, inspired and often brilliant. In the words of Modernist poet, playwright and author Guillaume Apollinaire, they offered works that were 'more cerebral than sensual'. They forced people to think instead of feel. They didn't see it as their mission to seduce people with prettiness or pleasant emotions. On the contrary, as the abstract painter

Barnett Newman wrote, 'the impulse of modern art was [a] desire to destroy beauty.'

Feeling was out, and thinking was in. Under the spell of the Modernist craze, the focus of artists shifted from the heart to the head.

Kazimir Malevich's *Black Square* and *Black Circle* (both painted in 1923)

SCULPTURE

OUT

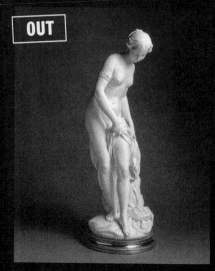

Etienne-Maurice Falconet, 1758

IN

Alexander Archipenko, 1912

POETRY

OUT **A Birthday**

My heart is like a singing bird
   Whose nest is in a water'd shoot;
My heart is like an apple-tree
   Whose boughs are bent with thickset fruit;
My heart is like a rainbow shell
   That paddles in a halcyon sea;
My heart is gladder than all these
   Because my love is come to me.

Raise me a dais of silk and down;
   Hang it with vair and purple dyes;
Carve it in doves and pomegranates,
   And peacocks with a hundred eyes;
Work it in gold and silver grapes,
   In leaves and silver fleurs-de-lys;
Because the birthday of my life
   Is come, my love is come to me.

Christina Rossetti, 1857

IN **Super-Bird-Song**

Ji
Uü
Aa
P' gikk
P'p'gikk
Beekedikee
Lampedigaal
P'p' beekedikee
P'p' lampedigaal
Ji üü Oo Aa
Brr Bredikekke
Ji üü Oo ii Aa
Nz' dott Nz' dott
Doll
Ee P' gikk
Lampedikrr
Sjaal
Briiniiaan
Ba baa

Kurt Schwitters, 1946

PAINTING

OUT

William Hazlitt, 1808

IN

Paul Klee, 1922

DANCE

OUT

Anna Pavlova, 1900

IN

Oskar Schlemmer, 1926

The Modernists despised all forms of 'ornamentation', whether flowery, overly descriptive writing or the frill and fancies of the decorative arts. Ornamentation was seen as banal, bourgeois, old-fashioned and dishonest. 'One is tired of ornamentations,' wrote Ezra Pound; 'they are all a trick.' As cultural critic Wendy Steiner writes: 'Manifesto after manifesto vilifies ornament: from Pound on imagist poetry to Hemingway on artistic honesty in prose.'

The Modernist movement swept through the arts like a revolution.

When it arrived in the world of architecture, it struck at its very foundations.

For thousands of years, since the days of Vitruvius and even before, it had been generally accepted that successful buildings should possess a combination of strength, utility and beauty (*Firmitas, Utilitas, Venustas*).

But now, one leg of Vitruvius's stool had been kicked away.

The joy one.

For Modernist artistic minds, the truth was what mattered.

And the truth wasn't pretty.

It was often scandalous, challenging and difficult.

But it was also interesting.

Which presents us with a puzzle.

How could the movement that produced the dazzling and brilliant art of T. S. Eliot, Virginia Woolf and Picasso also produce a worldwide epidemic of boring buildings?

To find out, we're going to meet someone who, arguably more than any other, pulled architecture into the world of Modernism and defined how this artistic movement would express itself in buildings. I'm going to use the thought and work of this man to tell the much greater story of how a generation of building designers began to see beauty in the mind-numbingly boring.

And why their ideas refuse to die.

 VENUSTAS

MEET THE
GOD OF BORING

Here he is, in his famous circular glasses, which would be copied and worn by many in the generation of architects he inspired, and which can still be seen on one or two faces in the business to this day.

He called himself Le Corbusier, the 'crow-like one'.

His real name was Charles-Édouard Jeanneret-Gris, and he was a child of the Modernist era. Born in Switzerland in 1887, he was almost certainly influenced by the same momentous and disturbing changes in the world as the poets, painters and storytellers that created the movement. Le Corbusier was surprisingly convinced of his own greatness, believing he was one of a small group of 'world historical individuals'. He also saw himself as an artist, writing in 1923 that 'architecture is the art above all others'.

LE CORBUSIER
Charles-Édouard Jeanneret-Gris

In the early twentieth century, great swathes of the world's urban areas were dangerous, dirty and diseased. Le Corbusier compared the typical family house to 'an old coach full of tuberculosis'. The ancient, winding streets of medieval city centres were overcrowded and, he believed, caused 'physical and nervous sickness' and a degradation of 'hygiene and moral health'.

He also thought them unfit for the fast-coming future in which people would be driving themselves about at incredible speeds in cars. He wanted to revolutionise buildings, towns and cities using Modernist ideas.

Just as Modernist artists wanted to throw out all the old rules of poetry, storytelling, painting and film, Le Corbusier believed that the architecture of the time was 'stifled by custom' and had to be radically reimagined. He liked to tell the story of his encounter with a fellow architect in Strasbourg in 1925, when he was serving on the jury of an international competition. One morning, the jurists were driven out of the city and into the fields and forests of the surrounding countryside. There, Le Corbusier poured praise on the perfectly straight lines of the canal and the railway track, which were 'inspiring and even poetical in the midst of this nondescript landscape'. One of the jurists protested at the vision that he seemed to be proposing – of a world of straight lines. 'Your straight avenue would seem interminable, one would die of boredom on it.'

Le Corbusier was 'astounded' when he heard this, replying, 'You have a car and yet you say that!' For the world-historical artist-architect, the other man was missing the point. Boring? This was about the future: 'It is essential . . . that motors can travel as directly as possible.'

Le Corbusier believed in the supreme importance of the function of the built world.

If a canal and a railway track operated at maximum efficiency when they were perfectly straight, then perfectly straight was how they should look. Perfect straightness was their truth, and truth was what mattered.

The same went for buildings. The truth of a building was what it was used for.

And how a building looked should represent its truth.

No ornament. No decoration. No sense of place.

The truth, and nothing more.

During his lifetime Le Corbusier wrote millions of words about his ideas in articles, pamphlets and books. His 'complete works' take up eight volumes, span 1,704 pages and cost nearly $1,000 (plus postage and packing).

Le Corbusier had so much to say for himself that other architects sometimes poked fun at him. Frank Lloyd Wright was said to have remarked, 'Well, now that he's finished a building he'll go write four books about it.' The French architect André Wogenscky once admitted, 'We cannot simply understand his books. They can be bewildering.'

I'm going to list seven of Le Corbusier's core beliefs. Because it's important that we fully understand his Modernist vision, I want to show you that these beliefs relate not just to the outsides of individual buildings but also to the streets, towns and cities that they combine to make up.

For the avoidance of doubt – and so you know I'm not exaggerating – I'm going to allow Le Corbusier to speak in his own words.

DECORATION SHOULD BE ABOLISHED

> [Decoration] is suited to simple races,
> peasants and savages . . . the peasant loves
> ornament and decorates his walls

LE CORBUSIER

Like many of his fellow Modernists across the arts, Le Corbusier scorned ornament and decoration. He wrote extensively about how he believed that buildings, inside and out, should represent the unadorned truth of what they were used for. Ornament and decoration were for simple-minded people. Modern, sophisticated men and women didn't need to be surrounded by complex visual frills and fussiness. They were above all that.

However, it's now known that love of decoration is part of human nature. Just as in many animals (most notoriously the peacock), our displays of beauty are rooted in the biology of sexual selection. Decoration is universal, and has been with us since the dawn of human time: all known human societies devote valuable resources to beautification. In a cave in South Africa, archaeologists have discovered a necklace containing at least sixty-five seashells shaped like teardrops, which would have been worn 75,000 years ago. Similar artefacts have been found in Algeria and also in Israel, where they were dated to 120,000 years ago. Other decorated shells, discovered in Indonesia, are thought to be more than 500,000 years old.

We've also been making interesting buildings for an astonishingly long period of time. Some of the earliest monumental buildings we know of were discovered in Ukraine in 1965, when a farmer who was extending his cellar found himself digging into a huge mammoth's jawbone. Excavations revealed four circular houses, each built out of dozens of interlocking jawbones and tusks. The science writer Gaia Vince describes them as 'remarkable, intricate constructions that took skilful planning and engineering to build'. Each house required 'an entire herd of mammoth bones' to construct, and would have taken a huge amount of time, energy and skill to make, with each skull weighing at least 100 kilograms and being enormously valuable, even then. These incredible buildings are thought to have been built around 20,000 years ago. They would have housed their own decorative objects: 'beautiful treasures: amber ornaments and fossil shells, transported as far as 500 kilometres from their source'. Earlier still is the Göbekli Tepe temple complex in Turkey. The ruins contain many sculptures and intricately carved megaliths, and the most ancient parts are thought to date to the tenth millennium BC.

Even the homes of Neanderthals, 65,000 years old, were decorated with stencils and paintings.

Modern science confirms this primal need for the visual interest that decoration can provide. Researchers have found that 'patterns in the absence of complexity repel us'. Studies suggest that people are happiest in an urban environment when they find something 'new and interesting to look at' roughly every five seconds. Most people find beauty in 'patterned complexity'.

The bare concrete walls beloved by Le Corbusier and other Modernists have been found to be hostile to humans precisely because of their lack of complexity. Through a neural process called thermoception, we subconsciously experience materials as if we're touching them. When we see materials that capture warmth, such as wood, we feel comforted. Concrete, metal and glass, on the other hand, tend to be experienced as cold and discomforting, and trigger an instinct to retreat.

The evidence is clear, and it comes from many sources: evolutionary history, neuroscience and psychology.

Ornamentation and decoration are human to their very core.

CITIES SHOULD BE BUILT AROUND STRAIGHT LINES

Le Corbusier believed that medieval-style
cities with winding roads were ugly,
didn't work and should be abolished.

'A modern city lives by the straight line . . .
it is the proper thing for the heart of a city.
The curve is ruinous, difficult and dangerous;
it is a paralysing thing' LE CORBUSIER

Le Corbusier was savage in his view of historical cities. He campaigned to have Paris's Right Bank, including the Marais district (which he described as 'the seventh circle of Dante's Inferno'), largely demolished and replaced with eighteen tower blocks, each 600 feet tall, arranged around a wide 'gridiron' system of roads.

He also insisted the Gare d'Orsay and the Grand Palais des Champs-Élysées 'do not belong to Architecture'.

This is what the centre of Paris would have looked like
if Le Corbusier had realised his plan.

Visualisation by Clemens Gritl

He even said that, in Rome, 'the uglinesses are legion'.

In 2021, the team behind the iconic *Rough Guides* travel book series asked their readers what they considered to be the world's most beautiful cities.

This was their top five:

1.

3.

2.

4. EDINBURGH

Le Grand Palais   A. P.
The Great Palace.

5. LONDON

Today, we can say without doubt that it isn't the old cities with medieval centres that are ugly and failed; it is boring places built by the Modernists.

The old cities were human.

BUILDINGS SHOULD BE DESIGNED FOR MASS PRODUCTION

Le Corbusier believed that buildings should
be easy to replicate, like machines or products.
Sense of place was not important.

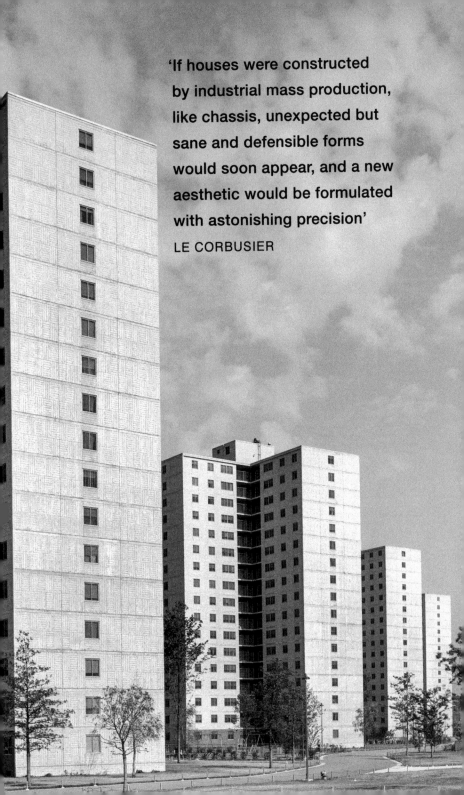

'If houses were constructed by industrial mass production, like chassis, unexpected but sane and defensible forms would soon appear, and a new aesthetic would be formulated with astonishing precision'

LE CORBUSIER

Actually, Le Corbusier was profoundly wrong: humans don't want to see the same building over and over again. They prefer variation.

This was demonstrated in 2012 by researchers from the University of Sydney in Australia and Uppsala University in Sweden. They wanted to find out what kind of urban scenes give people the benefit of psychological restoration – helping us to relax, concentrate and restore our depleted reserves of mental energy. They showed more than 200 participants different streetscapes, made up of different kinds of residential buildings. They discovered that greater architectural variation, both in the silhouettes of the buildings and in their surface details, increased psychological restoration.

BUILDINGS IN AMSTERDAM

Sense of place is important to people. Most people prefer buildings, and the places they make up, to look distinctive and to reflect the identity of their location.

A century after Le Corbusier, surveys have shown that people have a very strong or overwhelming preference for a 'more visually complex' style of building. The cities the largest number of people consider most beautiful, meanwhile, 'are intense, coherent and rich in architectural detail. Their "flavour" is local, not international.'

Sense of place tells us who and where we are.

Variation is interesting.

Monotony is boring.

Variation and sense of place are inescapably human.

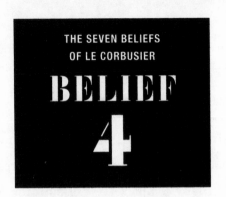

ALL BUILDINGS AND PLACES SHOULD BE DESIGNED PREDOMINANTLY WITH STRAIGHT LINES AND RIGHT ANGLES

'We rarely care to look at the silhouette of houses seen against the sky; the sight would be too painful. Throughout the town, in every street, the silhouette seems like a gash, a ragged, tumultuous line with jutting broken forms . . .'
LE CORBUSIER

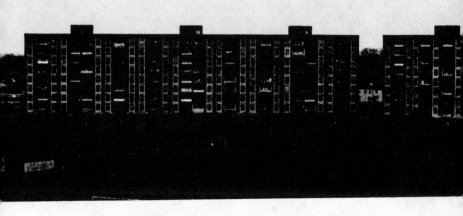

'Our emotion would be of a very different kind if the profile of the town seen against the sky . . . becomes a pure line . . . This is of the first importance' LE CORBUSIER

219

Le Corbusier's adoration for the right angle was so great that he spent seven years working on a book called *The Poem of the Right Angle*. What he didn't know was that most humans actually prefer some curves. In 2013, a team of scientists led by Dr Oshin Vartanian put people in a brain scanner and showed them a series of pictures of buildings. Some of these images were full of curvy details, whilst others were composed of straight lines and right angles. The participants were asked to decide whether they found each image 'beautiful' or 'not beautiful'. The scientists found that people were far more likely to find the buildings with some curves beautiful than the purely rectilinear ones. The brain scans gave a clue as to why. When the participants were observing the curved architecture, the scientists saw increased activity in areas of the brain that process emotional reward. We feel emotionally rewarded by curves' because they signal lack of threat, i.e. safety'. Meanwhile, brain scans by academics at the Harvard Medical School have shown that square and angled objects cause increased activity in the amygdala, which is the part of the brain that helps us deal with stress and fear. In another study, participants associated curvy shapes with 'quiet or calm sound', the smell of vanilla and a 'relieved emotion'. Angular shapes, constructed from straight lines, made them think of sour tastes, loud volumes, a citrus smell and the emotion of surprise. Elsewhere, researchers have found that people are much more likely to enter rooms that are curved rather than angular. Very young children have been shown to look longer at rounded shapes than they do angular ones (a behaviour that implies attraction). Travellers have been found to favour rounded architecture at airports. Even our evolutionary cousins the apes show a

If all that wasn't enough, Le Corbusier's love of grid patterns has also been found to be contrary to how human beings process the external world. Neuroscientists have found that our brains map our environment in angles of 60 degrees rather than his preferred 90 degrees: humans see the world not in a grid of squares, but in a lattice of hexagons:

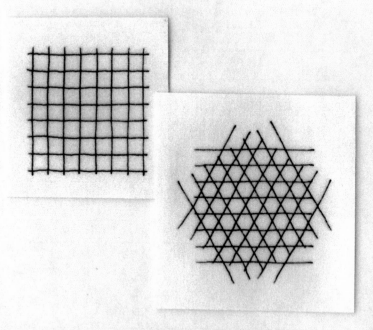

Consistent with this, most people would rather look at fractals than grids. Complex natural phenomena, such as coastlines, mountains and the frond of a fern, can be described in fractals.

Fractals can also be found in interesting buildings ranging from Hindu temples to Gothic cathedrals.

THE DETAILS OF THIS BUILDING ARE LIKE SCALED-DOWN VERSIONS OF THE WHOLE THING.

There are virtually no right angles in nature.

There's obviously a critical place for straight lines and rectangles in buildings. But when they're allowed to dominate, in the absence of sufficient complexity, they're inhuman.

Curves and fractals are human.

THE SEVEN BELIEFS
OF LE CORBUSIER

BELIEF
5

STREETS SHOULD BE ABOLISHED

'Our streets no longer work. Streets are obsolete.
There ought not to be such things as streets'
LE CORBUSIER

Le Café Fungus

OBSOLETE
BELIEF OF LE CORBUSIER

'Cafes and places for recreation would no longer
be that fungus which eats up the pavements of
Paris: they would be transferred to the flat roofs'
LE CORBUSIER

Earlier, we discovered how harmful the Kingdoms of Boring – so beloved of Le Corbusier and the Modernists – can be. When scientists examined Modernist-style housing blocks that were disconnected from the streets, they found that elderly people in the poor Hispanic neighbourhood of East Little Havana in Miami, Florida, were three times more likely to suffer from health problems (see p. 121). This was partly because these buildings lacked features that encouraged human connection.

Recent studies have found the design of streets to have similar effects. Researchers in Seattle found that passers-by are four times more likely to help strangers in need on 'lively streets filled with lots of small shops than on pristine, but essentially characterless blocks'.

Lead researcher Charles Montgomery explained: 'We think the kindness effect was a result of velocity. People are nicer to each other when they move more slowly and have time to make eye contact.' The old winding streets, so hated by Le Corbusier, are good for us. They encourage sociability. The wide, straight roads and empty, echoing plazas, characteristic of Modernist styles, are not. They also make us feel alienated and confused. Neuroscientists have discovered that the brain experiences any environment we enter as as an 'action setting'.

It processes place as a set of instructions, seeking answers
to the question: how do I interact with this location?
Where do I walk? Where do I sit? Where do I get shelter?
In which direction should I travel? The format of the
traditional street is crammed with answers to these
questions. It is a successful action setting. A Modernist
plaza or wide, empty boulevard is not.

Streets are to the human as the warren is to the rabbit: they look like they do because they reflect who we are. Humans are 'thigmotactic', which means we're a wall-hugging species.

PEOPLE STICKING TO THE WALLS OF A SPINNING DRUM

We're naturally drawn to – and naturally build – relatively narrow streets lined with walls of buildings. We prefer not to walk across wide-open empty plazas unless we're in a hurry, and will instead walk closer to the sides. Similarly, if there are benches available in the middle of a public space and along the sides, we tend to instinctively choose the seats on the sides.

PEOPLE STICKING TO THE WALLS OF A PUBLIC SPACE

Le Corbusier wanted the Right Bank of Paris to be a large grid system of wide roads between 36 and 122 metres wide. Surveys find that the most beloved streets are 11–30 metres wide. The exceptions, such as Barcelona's Paseo de Gracia or the Champs-Élysées in Paris, usually have their width broken up by avenues of trees.

The geometry of traditional-style streets makes us more social.

It makes us feel safe.

It gives the brain what it needs to act.

OLD CITIES AND SUBURBS SHOULD BE REPLACED BY HUGE BLOCKS SURROUNDED BY PARKLAND

'To conceive what such a vertical city would be like, imagine all this junk, which till now has lain spread out over the soil like a dry crust, cleaned off and carted away and replaced by immense clear crystals of glass, rising to a height of over 600 feet; each at a good distance from the next and all standing with their bases set among trees'

LE CORBUSIER

Le Corbusier fervently believed that the centres of older cities like Paris, along with their suburbs, should be demolished.

You don't need me to tell you that Modernist-style public tower blocks don't always make happy communities. Important research by urban design expert Alice Coleman found that these places were actively 'anti-community': full of dangerous corners and corridors, owned by no one, and graffitied, littered and fouled. The disconnection of people from each other as they live stacked on top of one another leads to an inevitable lack of 'eyes on the street' in semi-social spaces like front gardens. This further encourages antisocial behaviour, and the lack of human features discourages positive relationships from forming.

Most studies find that residents of these kinds of properties are less satisfied with their homes, more stressed, less optimistic and more depressed. According to Robert Gifford, a professor of psychology and environmental studies, the literature suggests 'that high-rises are less satisfactory than other housing forms for most people, that they are not optimal for children, that social relations are more impersonal and helping behaviour is less than in other housing forms, that crime and fear of crime are greater, and that they may independently account for some suicides'.

DODDINGTON AND ROLLO ESTATE

In 1971, filmmakers captured the lives and thoughts of people in London's Doddington and Rollo Estate, which was being built to house 7,000 people. The film *Where the Houses Used To Be*, featured the voices of many who'd been moved from traditional streets into this 'utopian' Modernist sky-city. One woman said: 'There's a lot to be said for giving people a decent place to live in. I don't know who designs them, I don't know who they design them for, or if they think we feel or think any differently than they do. There must be reasons why these architects build these flats in this hard, barrack-looking way. Because I'm sure they couldn't possibly like the design and the outlook of them themselves.

If they would've only consulted ordinary people who have to live in these places, what we would like. We do like the same things they enjoy. They like the outside of their places to look nice and so do we. We don't differ in any way to them. Surely in time somebody will learn to come and ask the ordinary people what they'd like.'

Boring estates are inhuman.

THE INSIDES OF BUILDINGS (THE PLAN) MATTER MORE THAN THEIR OUTSIDES

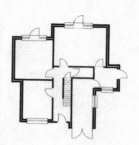

'The Plan proceeds from within to without;
the exterior is the result of an interior'

LE CORBUSIER

PESSAC, 1929

Le Corbusier believed that how a building looks on the outside should be the result of how it is designed on the inside.

And how it is designed on the inside should reflect its function.

According to Le Corbusier, buildings were machines for living and working in, and that was how they should look. Form should follow function. Anything that wasn't functional – any decoration, ornamentation, unnecessary curve or mere attempt at beautification – was a betrayal of its truth.

But here's the real truth of many of Le Corbusier's influential buildings: they've been rejected by the masses.

In 1929, he built a housing development in Pessac, in south-west France. 'I authorise you to put into practice your theories,' the developer told him. 'Pessac must be a laboratory . . .' But even when they were brand new, the buildings' appearance proved unpopular with ordinary people. The estate agents selling them even felt the need to address their boring appearance in the marketing material: 'The new look of this villa may perhaps raise doubts in your minds . . . The external appearance is not always pleasing at first sight.'

Incoming residents began modifying Le Corbusier's sparse designs, erecting fences around the roof terraces, adding planters, shrinking windows and placing walls around his beloved 'pilotis' – the pillars on which the buildings stood.

PESSAC ORIGINAL BUILDINGS

Today, local residents still struggle to embrace his Modernist vision. In 2015 the architecture writer Helena Ariza – a fan of Le Corbusier who was on a road trip through France and Switzerland, touring his work – found a number of the houses to be 'totally unrecognizable, transformed . . . Some interior spaces were divided to create new rooms, oblong windows were replaced by smaller ones that were square, terraces were covered, new sloping roofs appeared, car parks were removed.' Many of the houses 'were in very bad conditions, and some . . . even abandoned. It is not a very popular quarter among the inhabitants in Pessac.'

Despite this, in 2016, Pessac was listed as a UNESCO World Heritage Site.

WHAT THE RESIDENTS HAD DONE TO THEM BY 1967

Many architects, city planners and critics have held
Le Corbusier in the high esteem in which he held himself.

The architect and critic Peter Blake compared him
to Leonardo da Vinci and Michelangelo.

The architectural historian Charles Jencks called him 'arguably the greatest architect of the twentieth century'.

The architect and critic Stephen Gardiner called him a 'highly complex genius who led the twentieth-century architectural movement'.

On a warm summer day in 2009, I made a kind of anti-pilgrimage to a supposed Le Corbusier masterpiece. I was on a campervan holiday in Switzerland with my family, and managed to make a detour to a chapel – the Notre-Dame du Haut – that he had designed in Ronchamp, in the Franche-Comté region of north-east France. We pulled up in the car park in our Volkswagen Kombi van, and there it was.

One of the best buildings I'd ever seen in my life.

Completed in 1955, in the latter part of Le Corbusier's life, the small chapel was alive with both order and complexity. It had curved, white, leaning walls with lots of small windows in different sizes and positions and colours, and a stunning dark bending roof. Affordably built, it didn't look like a machine part from a production line, but rather a captivating creation of human fantasy. Inside the asymmetrical chapel, those varied deep windows cast a gentle light down into the dark interior, creating an atmosphere of mystery and wonder in the hushed quiet.

It was sublime.

What was this apparent schizophrenia that preached mass boredom but was also capable of such individual human brilliance? How did Le Corbusier have the ability to seemingly abandon everything he'd preached? As I stood there in awe, I had no idea.

But I had to admit, as a designer of individual buildings, the man might have been a genius.

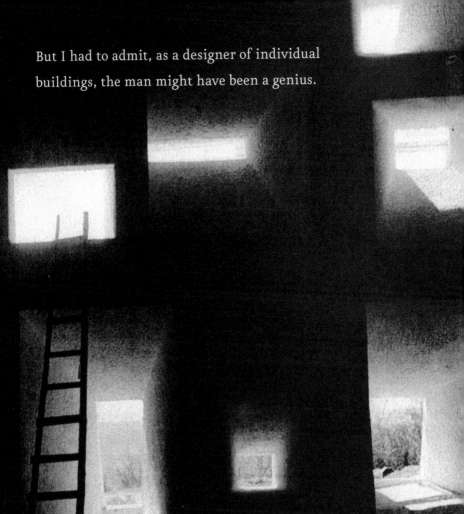

The tragedy for the world is that it wasn't stunning buildings like Notre-Dame du Haut that became widely influential. The ideas that Le Corbusier promoted so feverishly gave permission for repetitive order to utterly overpower complexity in the appearance of his buildings, and it was this look that spread like wildfire.

This is his celebrated 'Unité' block of flats in Marseilles, France, completed in 1952 – a repetitious, flat rectangle-for-living-in that inspired thousands of smoother, repetitious, flat rectangles-for-living-in all over the planet: in post-war Britain, the Soviet Union, Asia, post-colonial Africa and the Americas.

The architect and critic Kenneth Frampton called this building 'a breathtakingly heroic monument'; the architect Walter Gropius said that 'any architect who does not find this building beautiful had better lay down his pencil'.

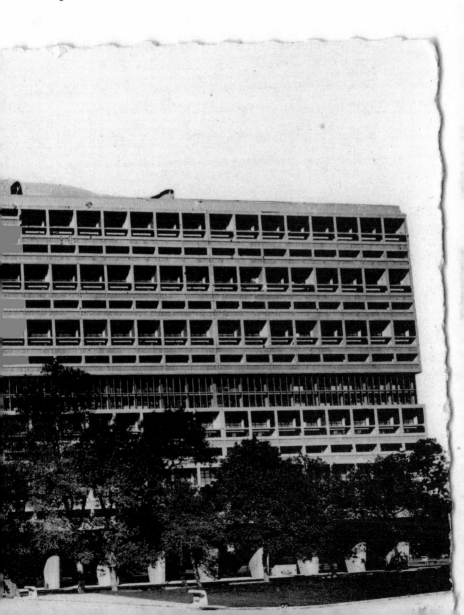

We should be wary of judging the Modernist building designers too harshly, with the smug benefit of hindsight. It's not hard to understand why Le Corbusier's idea of cities made of gigantic towers planted in open spaces was so compelling. Living and working up in the sky, surrounded by clean air and parkland, must have seemed like a marvellous and even inevitable vision of tomorrow.

The problems the Modernist building designers were facing at the time were real and urgent. Even before World War Two, the modern world had been rushing towards them at what must have seemed like an

exhilarating speed. The slums of the inner cities were often terrifying and overcrowded places, ridden with crime, poverty and disease. In 1921, the Beaubourg district of Paris – which Le Corbusier wanted to demolish – had 250 of its 276 houses designated uninhabitable because of tuberculosis contamination. Medieval city centres were also clearly not designed for a future of heavy motor traffic. And then World War Two did the work Modernists had often dreamed of: demolishing swathes of the old towns and cities of Europe.

Something new had to be born from the rubble.

WÜRZBURG, GERMANY. 1945

It's also important to remember that this story is much bigger than just Le Corbusier. I've been using him as a proxy to represent an entire movement because he's widely acknowledged to be the most influential Modernist building designer of them all, and left voluminous evidence of his every thought and theory.

But Le Corbusier was certainly not the only architect who applied austere Modernist ideas to buildings. Many others embraced the craze and designed similar structures. They too disregarded the criticisms of the public, who often complained that these buildings were brutal, plain, forbidding and anonymous. Like Modernist painters and sculptors, the architects privileged order over complexity and sought to represent pure forms – perfect squares and perfect rectangles, perfect right angles and perfectly uninterrupted lines.

Chief among them was Ludwig Mies van der Rohe. If Le Corbusier was the God of Boring, Mies (his almost exact contemporary) was the Virgin Mary. Whereas Le Corbusier agonised over whole-city planning, Mies focused on the individual building, often proposing giant rectangular structures covered in plate glass. He too sought to express modernity with a programme of ruthless austerity, forgoing curves in favour of straight lines and right angles; stripping away ornament and detail in favour of repetitive blankness at vast scales, imagining he was designing the ideal forms of tower blocks and campus buildings that others could then mass-produce. Mies helped popularise the phrase 'less is more'.

Overleaf are some Mies van der Rohe buildings that are celebrated as masterpieces.

Is less really more?

Or is it just what it says it is?

Mies van der Rohe

Carman Hall Apartments,
Chicago

IBM Building, Chicago

Lake Shore Drive
Apartments, Chicago

Lafayette Towers, Detroit

Weissenhofsiedlung, Stuttgart

Promontory Apartments,
Chicago

Wishnick & Perlstein Halls,
Chicago

Dirksen Federal Building,
Chicago

Mies's catchphrase is said to have been coined by an earlier pioneering Modernist architect: his creative 'godfather', Peter Behrens.

It is one of three beliefs that run through the ideology of the boring building designers, just as the Sign of the Cross, Hail Mary and Our Father run through Catholicism.

Louis Sullivan died in 1924.
Adolf Loos died in 1933.
Peter Behrens died in 1940.
Le Corbusier died in 1965.
Mies van der Rohe died in 1969.

Why have the ideas of these long-dead men stuck around?

How have they proved so incredibly resistant to rejection by multiple generations?

To find the answer, we must travel deeper into the minds of the boring building designers – and city planners – both past and present.

THE UNHOLY TRINITY

LESS IS MORE

PETER BEHRENS

FORM FOLLOWS FUNCTION

LOUIS SULLIVAN

ORNAMENT IS CRIME

(AFTER*) ADOLF LOOS

* Loos's influential lecture was
actually titled 'Ornament and Crime'.

HOW TO (ACCIDENTALLY)

A close friend of mine once attended a debate, held at an exclusive London club, between two big figures from the world of architecture. The topic was whether the public's opinions about buildings should matter. To my astonishment, he reported afterwards that, 'The general mood of the room was supportive of the idea that they wouldn't know enough to be worth listening to.' He told me: 'Most people thought, "Why would you ask them? What do they know?"'

This culture has protected the egos of elite building designers from the rejection of their work by the vast majority of the population. It says: *The masses don't like what we do because they're ignorant. We know better.*

It's a convenient fiction that allows them to dismiss the overwhelming evidence that most people just don't want what most building designers are making. It allows them to keep on building boring buildings, generation after generation, over and over and over again.

How did these people end up so separated from everyone else?

What do they see that the rest of us are so blind to?

Here's the surprising answer: Modernist architects think boring buildings are beautiful.

I found this out in 1999, when I was invited to a presentation about a new hospital building in east London to be designed by a famous architecture firm. Its designer stood on a podium, presenting his studio's proposals for this important new opportunity. Introducing his work in soft, charismatic tones, he described it as being reminiscent of a 'Tuscan hill town'. It sounded lovely. When the time came for him to show his drawings, I looked up eagerly for the big reveal.

The building was nothing of the sort. I thought to myself: 'That's no Tuscan hill town.'

I was confused. Where the architect saw a Tuscan hill town, I saw a huge ten-storey-high flat box with a few extra blocks sticking out of the front. To my surprise, it seemed I was the only one in the room who was seeing this. The audience around me was apparently charmed by this inhuman vision. After his talk, I sat there feeling bewildered. The romantic words didn't remotely match the design. Why wasn't he being laughed out of the room? In a sane world, surely it should be hilarious that this

boring, ugly building was being described as being like a 'Tuscan hill town'.

I realised something bizarre and chilling that day – something that's crucial to understand if we're to really grasp how the catastrophe of boring took over the world. When architects and non-architects look at buildings, they tend to see different realities. Modernist architects experience an alternative reality, in which their buildings are truly beautiful. And non-architect clients, scared of seeming ignorant or old-fashioned – and perhaps concerned that an alternative vision will be more expensive – give the benefit of the doubt to the building designer who they perceive as the expert.

Whilst many Modernist musicians, painters and writers of the twentieth century rejected the idea of representing beauty entirely, architects such as Le Corbusier took a slightly different course. Perhaps mindful of the fact they had clients to please and commissions to win, they declared their spare, blank, boring designs to be beautiful.

Here is the God of Boring himself explaining what, in his view, the simple, primary shapes – as commonly used in his buildings – make people feel (the CAPS are his):

'USE THOSE ELEMENTS WHICH ARE CAPABLE OF AFFECTING OUR SENSES, AND OF REWARDING THE DESIRE OF OUR EYES, and . . . dispose them in such a way THAT THE SIGHT OF THEM AFFECTS US IMMEDIATELY by their delicacy or their brutality, their riot or their serenity, their indifference or their interest; these elements are plastic elements, forms which our eyes see clearly and which our mind can measure. These forms, elementary or subtle, tractable or brutal, work physiologically upon our senses (sphere, cube, cylinder, horizontal, vertical, oblique, etc.), and excite them.'

Are Le Corbusier's buildings beautiful?

I happen to think that a small number of them are. But whatever my feelings or yours happen to be, it's hard to declare a building to be beautiful or ugly as a matter of fact. However, it is possible to note the weight of opinion. What kind of buildings are most people attracted to? As we've discovered, most people today and throughout history have been attracted to buildings that are interesting – that have details, three-dimensionality, ornamentation and a sense of history and place.

Then there was the research by neuroscientists, (see pp. 220–1) that confirmed most people find pleasure and reassurance in shapes with some curves, whilst finding purely angular, linear shapes threatening.

And yet most modern architects still seem to prefer their unadorned right angles, straight lines and flat surfaces.

How does their lust for boring come into being?

We humans are all so different, and when you see the work of painters, sculptors, musicians and writers, this difference is apparent. There's a huge variety of styles in the popular arts. But for some reason, many of the people who design our buildings end up liking the same flat boxes. Contrary to the view of critics who sometimes argue the world of building design has been taken over by sensationalist craziness, the reality is that most architecture firms create remarkably similar buildings in cities. You can barely distinguish which firm has done what.

How does this happen?

The answer lies in the process of becoming an architect.

THE CRIT

When I was in my late twenties, and still starting out
as a designer of buildings, I was invited to take part in
an event that's often feared among student architects.
During much of their seven-year training, a student's work
is assessed and challenged using what's called the 'jury
and crit' system. Dating from nineteenth-century Paris,
the 'crit' sees students having to pin up their work in front
of an audience of tutors, visiting experts and peers, and
then defend it as it's publicly critiqued. As professors of
architecture Rachel Sara from Birmingham City University
and Rosie Parnell from Newcastle University explain,
the crit is 'a rite of passage . . . that can be seen to mark
a student's progress from one status (uninitiated or
non-architect) to another (someone who thinks/acts like
an architect)'.

As I arrived at the architectural school, I had no idea about the work I'd be judging. I walked into a lecture hall to find seventeen nervous students preparing to defend their work to their tutors and me, the visiting expert. When I sat down I was told we'd be assessing their latest project. I wondered what it might be.

Had they been working on a block of flats in an environmentally sensitive location? An inner-city school on a tricky plot of land? A hospital on half the standard budget?

'What's the project?' I asked tentatively.

'A house for a one-legged man on the side of a cliff face in the zero-gravity context of the moon.'

I flashed back to my experience as a young teenager at the degree show, tripping over the twitching machine. At the time, I'd felt stupid for not understanding the work – that it was my failing for being naive and uneducated. But since then I'd had enough experience to realise that the stupidity wasn't mine. This was ludicrous. These hard-working students were having their time wasted.

I was witnessing a deluded intellectual elite giving birth to a new generation of itself, having become completely separated from the hopes, concerns and excitement of ordinary people. Especially troubling was the fact that this was a crit – an environment notorious for pushing students to think in certain ways. This is because humans have a natural copying instinct. It's long been known by psychologists that we're designed to unconsciously absorb the tastes and opinions of those we look up to. And the social dynamics that are embedded in the crit tend to magnify this evolved compulsion to mimic. The crit seems to be a place where young people undergo brain transplants as they learn how to think, talk, feel and act like architects.

Crits can be cruel and frightening. In 2017 *The Guardian* published a guide for architecture students on 'how to survive the crit', describing them as an 'emotional and theatrical assault course' that 'can feel like nothing more than a volley of abuse after weeks of hard work'. In an attempt to properly understand the experience, professors Sara and Parnell surveyed a group of students. They found the system was widely perceived to be flawed, and that it 'often fails to fulfil its potential as a place of constructive critical dialogue. Stress and fear are the most consistent experiences of the majority of students.' They asked students what the first word was that popped into their heads when they thought of the crit. Only 8 per cent responded with something positive; 42 per cent said relatively neutral words, like 'workload' or 'judgement', but the largest proportion of students thought of something negative – words like 'dread', 'fear', 'devastating', 'scary', 'stress', 'confrontation' and 'hell'.

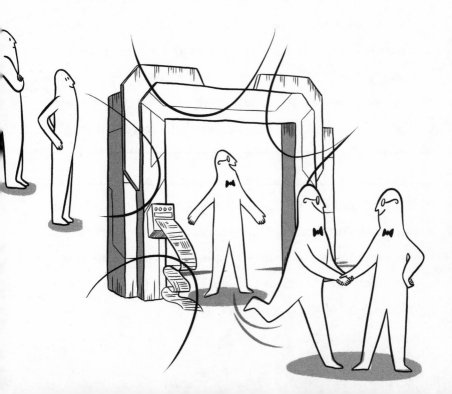

One recalled the time a superstar architect had joined a crit: 'Whole school turned out to watch each student be demolished by [the] guest. All [the] other tutors [were] too much in awe of him to step in and support their students.'

Of course, not all crits are bad. When I speak to the architects who work in my studio, some insist they didn't have experiences like these. I've no doubt there are universities that hold sessions that are positive and nurturing. But I worry that crits happen in front of a student's peers and are therefore potentially humiliating, and that their instinct won't be to discover their own aesthetic tastes – it will be to mimic those of their elders, who sit before them like judges. One student in Sara and Parnell's study confessed they were 'not thinking or caring about anything other than "is this what the tutor wants?"' Others described the 'negative potential' for crits to be a 'shaping tool' that 'inculcates students into the value systems and associated existing knowledge of the tutor-critics'.

In 2019, a group of architectural educators found that 'there is a great deal of evidence – both empirical and critical – to suggest that crits encourage conformity rather than creativity, and that they serve dominant cultural paradigms rather than the ideal of open-ended learning'.

It's surely no coincidence that it's exactly this – conformity, not creativity – that we see in the Kingdoms of Boring that smother the world.

THE THEORISTS

During a student's time at university, there's also,
in my opinion, too much emphasis on the work of elite
architecture theorists. Enthusiastic young students are
encouraged to read the works of thinkers like Jacques
Derrida, who express themselves on the subject of
architecture in language like this:

'We have here a figure of what some might be tempted to see as the dominant metaphorical register, indeed the allegorical bent of "deconstruction", a certain architectural rhetoric. One first locates, in an architectonics, in the art of the system, the "neglected corners" and the "defective cornerstone", that which, from the outset, threatens the coherence and the internal order of the construction. But it is a cornerstone! It is required by the architecture which it nevertheless, in advance, deconstructs from within. It assures its cohesion while situating in advance, in a way that is both visible and invisible (that is, corner), the site that lends itself to a deconstruction to come. The best spot for efficiently inserting the deconstructive lever is a cornerstone. There may be other analogous places but this one derives its privilege from the fact that it is indispensable to the completeness of the edifice. A condition of erection, holding up the walls of an established edifice, it also can be said to maintain it, to contain it, and to be tantamount to the generality of the architectonic system, "of the entire system".'

Many will be rewarded for writing and talking in this ridiculous way. Young architects who do so are actively continuing the tradition, created by the Modernists, in which their work is supposed to be 'more cerebral than sensual' – all about thinking impressively obscure thoughts, and appearing clever to each other, rather than exciting and engaging the public with extraordinary beauty, interesting ideas or pleasurable emotions. The outcome is that they begin to ignore what the heart says and consider only the head. Their focus moves away from actual people, and how they will experience and enjoy the buildings they'll one day make, and onto how it fits with their theories.

It was this process that led to the exhibition I witnessed when I was a teenager, with its unfathomable writings, abstract shapes and twitching machines, and to the students who'd spent weeks agonising over an overly hypothetical and irrelevant house on the moon for a one-legged man.

I sensed that if you challenged the academic leadership who were indoctrinating their students to instead ask them to design practical buildings that might actually please the general public, they'd probably accuse you of dumbing down the profession.

But I don't believe building designers who care about the public have dumbed down.

I believe these miseducated professionals have dumbed up. They are stuck in an intellectual cul-de-sac, spreading the same old inhuman values to each new generation of students that they teach. These students in turn become new versions of the same tutors, endlessly perpetuating the same approach.

All over the world, students coming out of this system have been imposing their ideas on the rest of the world and making buildings they believe have plenty to say but which are, most often, deadly boring.

The architectural education does its job.

It creates architects who think new versions of the same things that past architects have thought, and build the buildings that architects find beautiful.

But as we've seen, the problem is that the architectural profession and the public cannot agree what a 'beautiful' building actually is. This problem has been noted by the British psychologist Dr David Halpern (who is Head of the Behavioural Insights Team, a global social purpose organisation known as the 'Nudge Unit'). He decided to investigate how it came into being.

First, he had to understand whether the tastes of architects and the public really were all that divergent. He asked a set of architecture students and members of the public to rate the attractiveness of some photos of people and then of some buildings.

He wanted to know who agreed with whom.

On rating the attractiveness of people, the correlation between the architects and non-architects was 'extremely high'. When it came to beautiful people, everyone pretty much agreed with everyone else.

But when it came to the ratings of beautiful buildings, the correlation between the two groups was 'low and non-significant'. This meant that 'the architects all agreed with one another as to which buildings were attractive, and the non-architects all agreed with one another as to which buildings were attractive, but there was almost no correspondence between the two sets of preferences'.

What could be the cause of this stark divergence of tastes? Halpern discovered evidence of the indoctrination process that takes place during an architect's up-to-seven-year education. When he examined how the tastes of the students evolved, he found that the gap between their ideas of beauty and those of the general public grew wider the longer they'd spent at university. 'The difference between the first-year architects and the norm was relatively small (though still significant) but became markedly stronger among later-year students.'

This process of indoctrination leads to what Halpern describes as the designer's paradox: 'if an architect designs a building that he or she really likes, the chances are that the general population will dislike it for the same reason the architect finds it attractive.'

Halpern's research had uncovered evidence of exactly what I worry about: that architectural education can encourage not creativity, but blind conformity.

There's a word we use for this kind of indoctrination.

Brainwashing.

MODERNIST ARCHITECTURE IS A CULT

A cult is an insular community of people that separates itself from the wider world by following a unique set of beliefs and practices that are laid down by its leaders.

A cult's beliefs and practices must be radically different to those followed by ordinary people – it's exactly this difference that allows its members to believe they're separate and enlightened.

Only by strictly adhering to its arcane beliefs can cult members achieve acceptance and status within the cult.

This is why cults are recognisable both by the strangeness of their beliefs and by the conformity of their members.

Cult members don't look to the outside world for validation, because the outside world is ignorant and inferior. Instead, they look to each other and to the teachings of their leaders. They often have their own obscure tracts that must be studied if they are to achieve acceptance and enlightenment.

On p. 273 we encountered the strange and dense writings of Jacques Derrida. Compare that to the following piece of writing by Sun Myung Moon, founder of the Holy Spirit Association for the Unification of World Christianity, more commonly known as the 'Moonies':

'What happens to conflict when we enter the age of the level horizontal? The level horizontal is a place of tranquillity. There will be no conflict. It is like the tide, which after it has come in and reaches its highest point, forms a level horizontal where there is no motion, no conflict. After the moment of high tide has passed, the water begins to recede and resumes its motion. It recedes, but people who do not realise that the tide has come in and formed a level horizontal also do not realise it when the tide begins to go out. In time it goes all the way out and forms another level horizontal at its lowest ebb. Then it starts to come in again. This motion always forms an "X". It reaches a level horizontal and then comes down here. The level horizontal that was formed like this first moves to the left and once it has gone to the left it comes back and seeks for the right. Then the standards of "O" and "X" will all come together. But what has happened instead? This thing called "X" is not able to go through, and it doesn't work.'

Modernist architects study special texts to achieve enlightenment, and they also speak in their own special language. Learning insider language is a recognised part of the brainwashing process in any cult. It creates a sense of community, allowing members to identify each other and exclude unenlightened outsiders. It also helps to form the strange alternative reality that cultists live inside. Heaven's Gate called their home community in Wyoming 'the craft'; its kitchens were 'nutri-labs' and its laundries 'fibre-labs'. Followers of the Raëlism cult practise a laying-on-of-hands ritual they call the 'transmission of the cellular plan'.

The Modernist cult creates its bizarre boring-worshipping reality using its own esoteric language. Such as:

Fenestration (windows)

Soffit (ceiling)

Piloti (column)

Spandrel (side panel)

Curvilinear (curving)

Resi (residential)

Mullion (window bar)

Skin (outside of a building)

Cantilever (unsupported structure)

Envelope (outside of a building)

Vernacular (local tradition)

Genius loci (spirit of a place)

Façade (building face)

Charette (group design session)

Contiguous with (next to)

Enfilade (connected rooms)

Spatial enclosure (room)

Rill (stream)

Loggia (inset balcony)

Negative space (gap)

Typology (type)

Bifurcate (separate)

Parti (a building's organising principle)

Some people have called this kind of language
'archibollocks'.

It's not only architects who have been indoctrinated into the Modernist cult.

Lots of buildings around the world, whether boring or interesting, weren't designed by architects at all. I'm not an architect. Nor was Le Corbusier and nor was Mies van der Rohe. In the UK, the title 'architect' is protected by law. For a person to call themselves one, they must be approved by the Architects Registration Board. Section 20 of the Architects Act 1997 says the term can only be used to describe a person who's had the correct education, training and experience. (In 2018, an investigations officer at the Architects Registration Board sent me a threatening letter because someone else called me an architect. 'Continued use of the word may amount to a criminal offence and should be amended as soon as possible,' they said.)

A similar situation can be found in many other countries. Architecture is a protected profession in Thailand; in the US it's illegal to call yourself an architect unless you have been licensed by one of the states, a process requiring a degree in architecture, years of apprenticeship, and the passing of a multi-part exam with the American Institute of Architects. Colombians need a five-year degree and an exam pass; Italians need a master's degree in architecture, to have passed a multi-part exam called the 'Esame di

Stato' and to have registered with the Architects Registration Board; those in the Netherlands require a five-year degree from an accredited university or work experience before they can take an exam with the Architects Registration Bureau.

It's not easy, then, to call yourself an architect. Pretty much everywhere around the world it takes a person who has lots of time and resources to eventually earn the right to add the a-word to their email signature. This could be one contributing reason why, for example, just 6 per cent of all homes in the UK are actually designed by architects, whilst in the US it's thought to be 1–2 per cent.

But this doesn't mean that architects don't play a commanding role in the spread of boringness. They might not typically be used for the hundreds of thousands of cookie-cutter houses that are built up and down the UK in suburban areas, but each year they do work on the major projects in our towns and cities, as well as our public buildings including schools, shopping centres and hospitals. Architects lead the conversation. They're the influencers – their tastes and opinions and awards soaking down from the top and saturating much of the wider industry.

There's real pressure for everyone to conform to the cult's narrow, puritanical and austere vision of beauty. In recent decades there has been a particular trend towards praising straight lines, right angles and flat surfaces as being 'minimalistic'. It's fashionable to profess love for buildings that are 'simple' and 'subtle' and have 'clean lines'.

Minimalism can work wonderfully on a small scale. The iPhone is a modern masterpiece of minimalist technological design: its simplicity helps it to work so well for everyone. But buildings are not pocketable; they're the biggest objects it's possible to make. At these huge scales, 'simple' and 'subtle' and 'clean' become alienating and repetitive and inhuman. Minimalism becomes miser-abilism. The fashionable Marie Kondo approach to clutter might work inside a messy bedroom, but if you Kondo the outside of an entire block of condos, you're left with a giant rectangle of boring.

'EGO-DRIVEN'

ot timeless'   'NOT RIGOROUS'

'Overbaked'

'Crass'

'One-liner'

And yet an atmosphere of intellectual superiority surrounds such buildings, and this can make doubters scared to call out their dullness, in case other people – especially architects and architectural critics (who have trained in architecture) – think they're stupid. So they praise the dreary whilst gazing upon the interesting with a tutting eye, decrying it with a similar set of sniffy insults:

'Try-hard'

'Overworked'   'Fussy'

'Dumbed-down'

'Over-designed'

'Shouty'

'Vanity project'

Modernism is a bit like Heinz food: it comes in '57 varieties'. It has many different flavours and evolutions. If you're an expert in the building styles of the twentieth century, you might object that I'm ignoring other important currents and derivations of Modernism, such as Post-Modernism and Brutalism.

Here are some examples of these building styles:

POST-MODERNISM   BRUTALISM

If you've had the correct education, and have been trained to spot the difference, I've no doubt you're looking at these photographs and seeing radically different buildings.

But when I squint my eyes and look at them (other than a small number of exceptions), I still see too flat, too plain, too monotonous.

Different flavours of boring.

See p. 494 for captions.

In 1923, Le Corbusier complained that architecture had become 'stifled by custom'. One hundred years later, this has become true once again. Only now it's stifled by the customs of Le Corbusier's bygone era.

Modernists accuse their critics of being stuck in the past. But today it's the Modernists who are the merchants of pastiche – building and rebuilding their worn-out clichés from the last century. They're the ones who are stuck in the past; brainwashed into an obsession with an outdated fad that they still believe is modern, just because it has the word 'modern' in its name.

The cult of Modernism is keeping us stuck in an eternal twentieth century. It's the corpse of an aesthetic. It lays claim to a word that means 'now' but makes buildings that say 'then'.

So far we've looked at the culture of Modernist architecture and how it influences generation after generation of minds, through the power of education and the domination of certain tastes and opinions soaking down through an entire industry.

But the Modernist vision, and all its derivations, wouldn't have become stuck for so long if it hadn't been useful in other ways.

And when I say 'other ways', I mean one way in particular.

LOOK LIKE PROFIT?

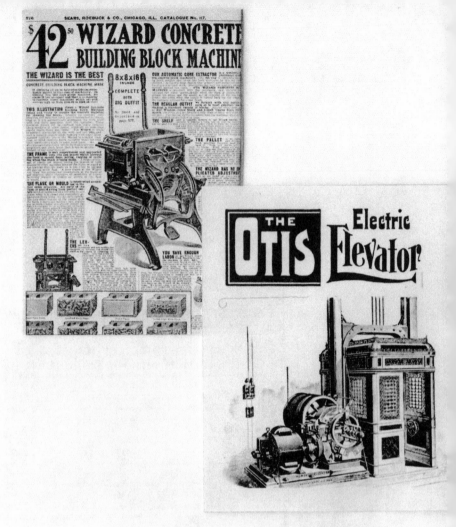

As the world began to industrialise in the nineteenth century, it also began to look more industrial. As the world became wealthier in the twentieth century, it began to look more like profit.

The Industrial Revolution triggered a tsunami-like shift from artisan building to mass production. The development of new materials and building methods inevitably affected the size, shape and style of buildings. New ways of working iron, forging steel and reinforcing concrete meant structures could now be far taller; the ability to construct buildings from steel frames instead of load-bearing brick walls meant that you could cover entire outer walls in glass; the creation of the elevator meant those higher floors could be easily accessed; the invention of electric lighting and air conditioning meant people no longer had to be so close to windows, so buildings could be deeper.

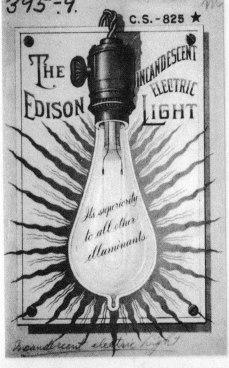

Global innovations such as the spread of new transport networks also had an effect. For the architect and professor Adam Sharr, the arrival of the railways across Europe and North America 'captured people's imaginations' – including those of famous painters such as Claude Monet,

who depicted a Parisian train shed in his *Gare Saint-Lazare* (1877). Utilitarian styles that openly displayed their technological prowess and internal structure seemed futuristic and thrilling – a fantastic example of this was the Eiffel Tower (1889).

AND THEN THERE WAS

WORLD WAR TWO.

Over a million houses and flats were destroyed in Britain, whilst 70 per cent of housing in Germany and 19 per cent in Japan was devastated. In the post-war years, not only had millions of people been bombed out of their homes, a baby boom was in motion and the global population was rapidly growing. There was a sudden need for housing that was cheap and easy to put up. But it didn't seem like there was enough time to build houses brick by brick with thought and care. Through necessity, mass production and industrial techniques had to be embraced. By the use of easily available prefabricated materials, buildings could be erected at incredible speed.

Most people didn't want to think about yesterday, and didn't want their homes, hospitals, schools and offices to look like yesterday either. The past was unwanted, and so was its building styles.

Aus Sachsen für Berlin!

ALLE BAUEN MIT
AM NATIONALEN AUFBAUPROGRAMM

According to the architect Christoph Mäckler, in Germany, 'simply putting two columns next to each other was considered fascist'. His father, the master builder Hermann Mäckler, was an active participant in Germany's Modernist reconstruction, and once proposed that Frankfurt's cathedral should be given a flat roof. His generation was so desperate to create new and 'honest' cities, his son has said, that they forgot that liveable cities are 'about beauty, and beauty is linked to the history of the place you are building in'.

Germany's post-war rebuilding was frantic, with as many as 714,000 apartments being constructed in a single year. In the decade and a half following the end of the war, over 5 million flats were built in West Germany alone. 'The task seemed endless and money was everywhere,' says an account of that period in the German publication Der Spiegel. 'The outcome, however, was less than impressive – mass-produced buildings that compared poorly with the pre-war buildings which they replaced.' Many new communities that sprang up were directly inspired by Le Corbusier's Modernist vision of the ideal town and city. 'They were intended to provide "clarity" rather than the "confusion" of the historical city. Unfortunately, the clean new suburbs and satellite towns didn't result in a better quality of life. Instead, the sterile environments elicited feelings of loneliness and boredom. Indeed, many of those who moved to these soulless ghettos were soon pining for the familiar, chaotic confinement of their former cities.'

The fever for these new Modernist dreamworlds reached such a pitch across the broken towns and cities of Europe, that it wasn't only buildings on bomb sites that were created in the boring style. In the UK, swathes of Victorian, Georgian and Edwardian housing were dismissively declared 'slums' and knocked down, rather than being modernised with features such as indoor plumbing. Exactly what did these pre-war buildings do to deserve such a fate? As the architecture writer Paul Finch has pointed out: 'Slums are not about the house, they're about the number of people in the house. If you put fifty people in a Georgian terrace, it's a slum. If it's a family of four, it's a luxury villa.'

Even putting aside the dreary look of the new buildings that replaced them, many were not as good at the simple job of being a functional home. 'There's no denying there were some bad technical consequences,' Paul says. 'For example, condensation and mould in local authority blocks, because somebody had forgotten research that'd been done in the late 1940s that found that when you introduce strict insulation systems, if you're not thinking about your ventilation, you create conditions in which everything becomes sodden.'

In the second half of the twentieth century, new Modernist building styles swept through Europe and the rest of the world. As decade followed decade, boringness spread over the continents like a beige fog, suffocating millions in its aggressive nothingness. Wherever new building happened, the Modernist so-called International Style was usually chosen. Old buildings and streets and neighbourhoods were demolished and tower blocks and estates were built, which were often located away from the amenities of the crowded city centres.

The iconic Scottish comedian Billy Connolly lived through this revolution, and has vividly described his feelings about his own street in Glasgow being demolished. In 1956, he and his family were forced to move from their city-centre flat to a new housing estate 5 miles west of the city.

He recalls tens of thousands of Glaswegians being 'told we were living in slums and that we had to go. So we went – to a different kind of slum in the country called Drumchapel. Now we all had indoor plumbing. The problem was, we had fuck all else. When they took us there, there were no amenities. It was a crime to move thousands of people to a housing estate with no cinemas, no theatres, no cafes, no shops, no churches, no schools – just houses. Being moved to a new house is a good thing, but not if that's all there is. So you'd get up in the morning, go to your work, come back to your house and go to sleep.

There's something nasty about it. It was a dirty trick played on us . . . Even as a boy I knew that cafes, cinemas and community were the key to a sane life. If a place has none of those things, a dullness descends. A kind of anger develops. And if you have no way of articulating that anger you just lash out. And the architects of this brave new world? Town planners in Georgian houses.'

But there was nothing Connolly, or any of the other tens of thousands of forcibly relocated Glaswegians, could do about it.

The future was here.

And the future was boring.

BILLY CONNOLLY

This

TORONTO, CANADA

TUNBRIDGE WELLS, UK

NEW YORK CITY, UNITED STATES

BECAME THIS

All over the world, we place an enormous value on money. In 1967, 45 per cent of US college students said it was 'important to be well off financially'. By 2004 that number had climbed to 74 per cent. A 2015 survey by psychologists found money to be the leading cause of stress in America.

But it's not just in the West. A major global survey by Ipsos found the populations most likely to agree they feel 'under a lot of pressure to be successful and make money' are those of China, South Africa, Russia, India, Turkey and South Korea. Similarly, it's the people of China, India, Turkey, Brazil and South Korea who are 'most likely to measure their success by what they own'.

When money-making becomes the principal way to assign value to things, we use it as a lens through which to view the world and the scale on which to measure it.

How do we judge the success of a building in the twenty-first century?

By how much it costs to build?

By how much rent it earns its owners?

Or how much money it makes when it's sold?

Buildings are a gold mine. Actually, they're better than a gold mine. According to the urban geographer Samuel Stein, the globe's total real estate is worth $217 trillion, which is '36 times the value of all the gold ever mined. It makes up 60 per cent of the world's assets, and the vast majority of that wealth – roughly 75 per cent – is in housing.'

So, buildings and money have become inextricably linked. People who want lots of money buy land and build things on it. All over the world, wherever we've seen money become a dominant value, we've seen the rise and spread of buildings whose success or failure is judged mostly on how much profit they make.

One of the countries in which this has very obviously happened is my own. Paul Morrell was the UK government's first chief construction adviser and has spent a lifetime arguing that we should stop viewing the success of buildings principally through the lens of profit. He told me that the problem of boring buildings is 'driven first of all by most people not having any idea where value lies in a built asset, including by the development and construction industry itself. If it's an office building, you want brain power out of people, don't you? So that's where your value should lie: what kind of building creates the most creative power?

In a hospital it should be patients healed; in a prison it should be the number of inmates who go back into society and don't reoffend. The question shouldn't be "How many square feet can I get away with stacking on this site for the least amount of money?" It should be "What works?"'

One reason Modernism endures today is because it's perfectly compatible with cheapness. It's the ideal cover for any building-makers who are driven to place the value of money over the experience of those who'll have to live with what they make.

THE GOD OF BORING IS ON THE SWISS BANKNOTES

THE WIN-WIN (LOSE-LOSE)

The sad fact is, boring buildings are more profitable in the short term. It's unquestionably cheaper to make buildings that are flat, square and repetitive. Most property developers love to strip out as much 'unnecessary' cost from their designs as they can get away with. The architectural profession calls this 'value engineering'. It's a mindset that tends to look at interesting, creative features – a curve over a doorway, some detailing on a wall – and instead sees needless expense that could be erased to save money.

Value engineering conspires with the Modernist cult by giving these developers a seductive story to tell: their plain buildings are not boring but 'enlightened', and they show the apparently inarguable qualities of simplicity,

subtlety, understatement and clean lines. And so, by ruthlessly stripping out anything interesting, property developers not only become wealthier, they also get to feel intellectually superior. It's a win-win for them. (But a lose-lose for everyone else.)

Below is a house in north London. It happens to be the house where the singer Amy Winehouse used to live, just around the corner from my first studio.

Let's try value engineering it.

Which house do you prefer? The original one on the far left, with the decorative details? The one on the far right? Or one in-between?

RISK AVERSION

Another important factor in the spread of boringness is that a building designer is often legally liable for their building for decades after it's been built. Therefore it's in their interest to be cautious. So instead of designing their own unique windows, for example, they'll choose a

standard available 'window system' from a specialist manufacturer. When they do this, legal liability for the windows themselves shifts from the architect to the manufacturer. The same is true of the other major pieces and parts that go into making a modern building, from the walls to the lifts. They're seldom designed specially for the project, but instead are a collection of standard 'systems' or 'products' put together to form the building. They're therefore designed to be as useful as possible to as wide a range of projects as possible, which means they're typically bland and uniform in appearance.

Buildings that use these kinds of products and systems, such as curtain walling, are frequently less sustainable. Because, just like other types of mass-produced consumer products, they are hard to repair. They tend to be only replaceable or repairable by their original manufacturers, who almost inevitably stop producing the specific product after ten years or so, or even completely go out of business after twenty or thirty years.

PROPERTY AGENTS

Another incredibly powerful force in shaping the world around us, property agents tell the developers what they'll be able to sell or rent. So the true 'customers' of the developers and their building designers tend not to be the specific families who will be buying and living in the flats and houses (and certainly not the millions of us who will be forced to experience the outsides of these buildings), but the property agents who are lumping all the potential customers together. And because there is generally such a shortage of property globally, it's a seller's market – scarcity makes values go up even if the quality is low. This is why the commercially driven people who pay for new buildings tend to focus on the insides of spaces. They don't have to care too much about the outsides because most properties will sell anyway, regardless of how dull the outsides appear.

If I were to tell a property agent that they should care more about what homes look like on the outside, they'd probably say: 'Why? I sell every single home I'm given.' It's scary to realise that there's so little financial incentive to spend time and money making the outsides better.

DESIGN AND BUILD CONTRACTS

It's not always true that architects are in charge of the design of major public building projects. These days it's increasingly common for clients to ask for building companies to lead them and essentially appoint and control the architect. This is often the case with state-funded projects, as local authorities perceive their financial risks to be reduced by a number of factors, including limiting the control of building designers. These 'design and build' contracts are seen as being simpler for the client to manage, but the priority is often inadvertently time and money, and creative quality almost always suffers.

....

SIGNED

....

WITNESSED BY

THE EFFICIENCY OBSESSION

The building profession talks constantly about 'efficiency'. This is the difference between how many square feet of a building you can build, with its associated costs, versus how many square feet you can actually sell or let to somebody. In a housing project, for example, the marketing team will say that they can't sell the shared corridors, so the pressure is on to have the shortest and narrowest corridors possible.

Efficiency also means maximising the perceived internal room size, which inevitably encourages external boxiness. Land is valuable, and sites usually have straight boundaries that you aren't allowed to overhang or build over. As a height limit is almost always imposed by the city's authorities, the developer and building designer are incentivised to build out to the maximum width possible, so they understandably try to use up every millimetre of space. This creates a tendency for everything to be pushed out, flat and square:

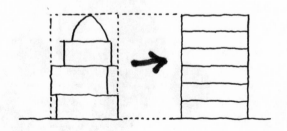

Imagine there's an invisible and extremely flat glass box around the edges of every site. If you want to get the maximum 'efficient' internal area to sell, you have to squash away any three-dimensionality on the outside until the surface of the building is as flat as possible against that invisible line of glass. Similarly, from the inside, a space you're selling looks biggest when the windows and their frames are pushed out as far as possible within the openings of the walls. The outcome of this is that the glass becomes almost flat, and aligned with the external surface of the wall:

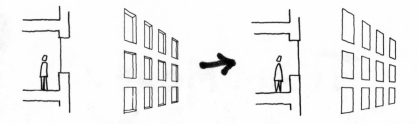

Sadly, windows almost always look best for all of us in the streets of a city when they're not just flat and aligned with the outside surfaces of a building. They look best when they're pushed inwards, creating three-dimensionality and a play of light and shadow, and helping to break down the monolithic boxy feel of a building.

Who should win? The small handful of people who see this new building from the inside? Or the millions who'll see it from the outside? It's like a tug of war between the insides and outsides of buildings, with the selfish forces of money the likely winner on the inside, and the public the loser on the outside.

As we learned earlier, Vitruvius famously wrote that buildings should have *firmitas*, *utilitas* and *venustas*. For centuries, we built buildings that were indeed strong, useful and beautiful. But now that beauty has largely fallen away, what virtue might a modern Vitruvius speak of?

Probably not beauty but efficiency. 'Efficient' is exactly how new buildings all over the world appear today. Their highest value is not focused on the people who'll see and use them every day, but on those who'll make money from them.

Why do so many of the world's new buildings look like greed? Because the ultimate customer in our capitalist world is not the public.

TEAM PUBLIC

REGULATIONS

It's not just that many modern buildings look like money.
They also look like regulations and codes. Clearly, we do
need regulations to make sure that buildings are safe,
fair and don't fall down. But regulations mustn't prevent
them from being joyful. Building designers are increasingly
forced to negotiate a vast and bewildering quantity of
rules that can dictate everything from where light switches
can be placed to the slant of rooftops.

The architects Liam Ross and Tolulope Onabolu investigated
the impact that regulations and codes have on building
design. One regulation they analysed was Standard
8213-1:2004, Design for Safety in use and during Cleaning
of Windows:

'This regulation recommends that windows should be maintainable from within – without the use of a stepladder or cleaning devices and without stretching – by women in the 64–75 year age range. Additionally, the regulation recommends that window size is limited to meet a maximum overhead reach of 1,825 mm, and 556 mm while reaching outside.'

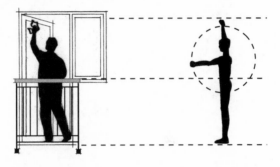

They found that this single regulation had a 'profound impact' on the buildings that they looked at in Edinburgh, where it had led to a widespread outbreak of small, mean-looking windows – many with flat, steel, prison-bar-style 'Juliet' balconies to protect inhabitants from falling. Ross and Onabolu concluded that 'most British architects consider architecture to be over-regulated, stifling innovation and creativity and leading to standardised and monotonous designs', and that 'much of contemporary architecture resembles the clauses of building regulations set in bricks and mortar'.

PLANNERS

Since at least the 1950s, many city planners have fallen into the Modernist mindset. They've encouraged and approved thousands of inhuman projects, and conspired in the demolition of many districts of interesting buildings. But it's not true that planners always act on the side of the dull. I've met some who are frustrated themselves and have even said to me, 'Why do the designers keep giving us this rubbish?' A major project of mine was

made more interesting after an intervention by the planners at the London Borough of Camden. Coal Drops Yard in London's King's Cross is a shopping district created by redeveloping two Victorian warehouses that once stored Yorkshire coal. We chose to rebuild the existing roofs in a way that sinuously joined the two warehouses together. But when we presented our designs to the Camden planners, they rejected them.

'You're not acknowledging that they're two separate buildings,' they said. We left the meeting comforting ourselves by saying they were narrow-minded and wrong. But then I stopped and asked myself and my team, 'What if they've got a point?' We then developed a new version where, instead of completely blending the buildings, we kept them separate, making them reach out and

appear to kiss in the air. If it hadn't been for Camden's planners, the finished place would have been a lot less inspiring to visit. Of course, different regions of the world have different kinds of planners and planning systems and cultures. However, in general, most building designers see planning as an annoying hurdle they have to jump over. But we forget that, wherever we are, the system is supposed to represent the voice of the people. A humanized planning system would understand and fight for the feelings of ordinary passers-by.

WHAT'S DIFFERENT ABOUT INTERIORS?

This book is about the outsides of buildings, but it's interesting to look at the rise of a new profession that emerged in the last century as compensation for buildings that were otherwise losing their ability to engage the emotions of their users. Once, architects would pride themselves on designing beautiful integrated interiors. Building designers like Frank Lloyd Wright and Charles Rennie Mackintosh created insides that were filled with visual complexity and joy.

Although today's building designers have to care a lot about the sellable size of their interiors, they have largely lost the art of thinking about how the details of the rooms they create will make people feel. When they do try, the results are often half-hearted. The drive for never-ending visual simplicity tends to make places that are too plain. Building designers have unwittingly surrendered their understanding of the insides of buildings, to the point where they no longer know how to infuse them with mood and feel.

So, the task of mastering mood and feel has increasingly been taken over by interior designers and artists.

I learned this the hard way when I was first commissioned to design a hotel building. When my client asked which interior designer I'd like to work with on the insides, I dropped a hint that my own studio could do it but was immediately cut short and told that 'architects don't understand mood and feel'. This seemed so shocking when it was voiced with such brutal clarity. Even though I'm not an architect myself, and even though I instinctively knew what he was saying was true, I still felt a bit defensive of the profession I align myself with. As I employ more than 200 people, many of whom are architects, it was almost like a stranger had insulted a family member. I remember going back to my team in London and sitting everyone down and saying that this had to be our own challenge – to understand mood and feel, whether on the insides or outsides of buildings. We had to learn how to engage the emotions, and not just the minds, of the people we designed for.

Sadly, if you want to see human-centric design in most modern buildings, you have to go inside them. Some of the most interesting, emotionally satisfying places you can find today are the insides of restaurants and hotels. This is because the ultimate customers of these places aren't developers or agents, but members of the public who simply wouldn't turn up if they weren't made to feel good.

The interiors pictured over the next few pages are literally sensational: they're designed to create sensations when you walk through them.

They hold emotion as a primary function.

They are human places. And they hold valuable lessons for how we might be able to humanize the outsides of buildings.

Miquel Barceló, ceiling decoration for the UN Human Rights & Alliance of Civilizations Room, Geneva

Yayoi Kusama, Louis Vuitton & Kusama concept store, London

Ashley Sutton, The Iron Fairies bar, Hong Kong

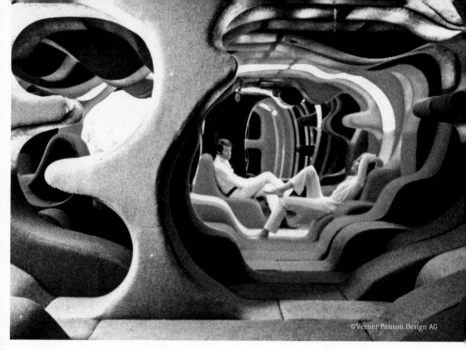

Verner Panton, *Fantasy Landscape* installation at 'Visiona 2' exhibition, Cologne

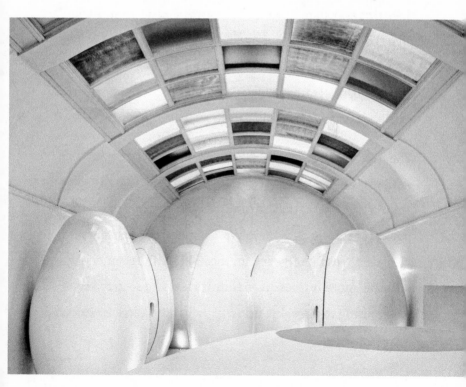

Mourad Mazouz and Noé Duchaufour-Lawrance, toilets at Sketch restaurant, London

So what can we do about fixing the global catastrophe of boring?

I once spoke to a senior medical adviser to the UK government about the need to build better hospitals. She told me, 'If you want to make a better hospital environment, you have to create patient pull.'

Patient pull?

It was such a powerful expression. She was telling me that politicians will only respond when the patients as a group expect and demand it. Paul Morrell told me something similar: 'A politician's first thought would be, "In what way does this translate to votes?" I'm afraid to say that if you give them a choice between one hospital that works or two that don't, they'll build two that don't, because it's the vote winner: beds created, not patients healed – quantity (that's easily measurable), as opposed to quality (which isn't).'

The hard truth is that the buck of boring doesn't stop with architects. Whether or not they're sensitive to the emotions of users, they're often the victims of a vastly more powerful system of money, bureaucracy and government. And even when they want to, they're often prevented from building more interesting buildings because society keeps on choosing to see value principally in cost and efficiency.

Until boring buildings become a vote-loser for politicians and councillors, and we begin insisting to planners and developers that we must have better buildings in which to live, work, learn and heal, the catastrophe of boring will continue its conquest of the world.

That means that society has to change.

WE MUST ADJUST OUR VIEW.

WE MUST ACKNOWLEDGE THAT INHUMAN BUILDINGS ARE CATASTROPHIC FOR HUMANS AND OUR PLANET.

WE MUST STOP SEEING THE WORLD, AND WEIGHING ITS VALUE, THROUGH THE LENS AND SCALE OF MONEY.

WE MUST GET ANGRY.

WE ARE WHERE THE BUCK STOPS.

A NEW MOVEMENT TO RE-HUMANIZE OUR WORLD MUST BEGIN.

PART THREE

How to re-humanize the world

CHANGING HOW WE THINK

CHANGING HOW WE THINK

A truly rational human world is one that doesn't look like efficiency or profit or perfected machines.

It's a world that reflects who we are as a species, in all our incredible diversity, fluidity, history and eccentricity.

It's a world of never-ending interestingness and multiplicity.

A MOUSE BUILT THIS

A CORAL POLYP LIVES HERE

Have you ever seen an animal live

A CADDIS FLY BUILT THIS

A SPIDER LIVES HERE

A BiRD BUiLT THiS

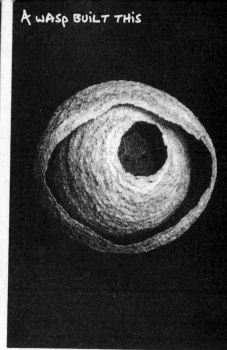

A WASp BUiLT THiS

in a boringly designed home?

A SNAiL BUiLT THiS

(BUT A CRAB LiVES HERE NOW)

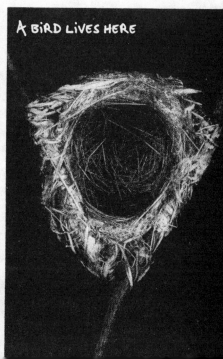

A BiRD LiVES HERE

Does an owl or a termite or a badger or an oyster live in a structure devoid of visual complexity?

Until about a hundred years ago, neither did we.

But I'm not proposing that every new structure we put up has to be a Casa Milà or a Marine Building. Neither do I want to see street after street lined with houses shaped like pineapples, ice cream cones or eyeballs.

I'm suggesting something far more simple and far more modest: that all new buildings that are visible to the public should be interesting.

That when we pass by them every day, we should feel something better than nothing.

I'd like to propose a simple rule . . .

THE HUM

A BUILDING SHOULD BE ABL
FOR THE TIME

NIZE RULE

O HOLD YOUR ATTENTION
AKES TO PASS BY IT.

As modest as this rule might sound, it's being failed today by building designers all over the world.

Reversing this global blandemic is going to take a radical shift in thinking.

I've no interest in telling people precisely how buildings should look, and even if I did, nobody would listen.

I'm simply arguing that there should be enough interestingness to engage a passer-by for the short time it takes them to experience it. I don't want to replace one aesthetic cult with another.

What we need isn't more conformity, but more creativity.

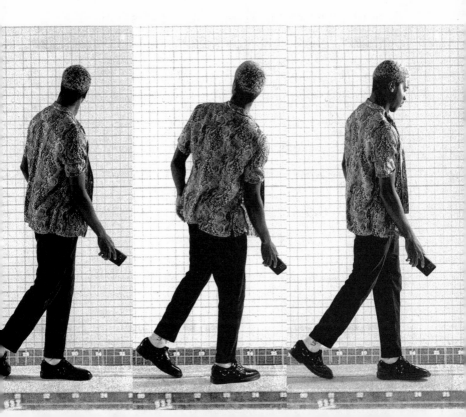

If you're particularly sharp-eyed, you might have noticed that the rule doesn't specify how the person who is passing by the building happens to be travelling. They might be on foot, in which case they'll be especially affected by its appearance close up. But they might be passing by on a bike or in a car or a bus. For these people, the building must succeed in being interesting even when they're whizzing past its finer details.

And when I say 'passing by', I mean the whole experience of doing so. No matter how we're travelling, we never have just one experience of a building. Shopping centres and apartment blocks don't suddenly appear, leaping out in front of us like ghouls on a ghost train. First we see them from a distance and experience them one way. Then we see them from across or down the street and experience them another way. We then see them in a different way again when we're close to them.

A building that can't hold a person's interest from three distances has got a problem.

It should unfold like a fractal, revealing more of itself the closer you get to it.

CUT OUT AND KEEP

THE
HUMANIZE
RULE.

A BUILDING SHOULD BE ABLE TO HOLD YOUR ATTENTION FOR THE TIME IT TAKES TO PASS BY IT.

In order to pass the test this rule sets, a building must be interesting from three distances:

1. City distance
of over 40 metres

2. Street distance
of around 20 metres

3. Door distance
of about 2 metres

CITY

STREET

DOOR

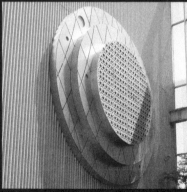

CITY

DISTANCE INTERESTINGNESS
40 METRES

If we stand around 40 metres away from it, even
an extremely large building can usually be seen in
its totality. We don't have to look up and down or
left and right to grasp it. It sits in our vision entirely.
We'll notice its overall shape and colour and whether
it moves in and out three-dimensionally. When we
experience a building in this way, it's like looking at
a whole object – like a sculpture or a piece of jewellery.
And just like a sculpture or a piece of jewellery,
that distant building has the power to make us
feel something.

Alwyn Court, New York. Harde & Short, 1909

CITY

STREET

DOOR

STREET

DISTANCE INTERESTINGNESS
20 METRES

When you see a building from across the street, you'll probably find it harder to take the whole structure in without moving your head. You might not be able to see its roof without really trying. But the building will start to show itself in greater detail. If it's a human building, there's likely to be complexity and interest in the patterns that exist on its surface. You'll begin to notice more of its three-dimensionality, texture and personality. It might also announce its use in ways that are whole-hearted and celebratory, rather than just having a logo stuck above a window or a sign placed next to a door. There should be enough visual interest to trigger your curiosity and make you want to look again.

John Lewis, Leeds. ACME Architects, 2016

CITY

STREET

DOOR

DOOR

DISTANCE INTERESTINGNESS
2 METRES

The door distance is where a building's materials, details and craftsmanship really impact you with their presence or hit you with their absence. When I'm looking at a building from close up, I sometimes think of my days as a student, drawing objects at the British Museum. Before I sat down with my pencils and sketchbook in front of something like an Egyptian chair, I'd first make sure that whatever I was looking at had sufficient complexity to make it worth drawing. A properly complex object is one that rewards your attention. The more you look at it, the more it reveals itself to you in layers of patterns, as well as little stories that you begin to make out about the item's makers and users and the era and culture of its creation. Exactly the same is true of buildings. Great buildings are worth the bother of drawing and experiencing from close up. Boring buildings are not.

15 Clerkenwell Close, London.
Amin Taha at Groupwork Architects, 2017

CITY

STREET

 **DOOR**

The Parkroyal Collection hotel on Pickering Street, Singapore, designed by WOHA, is a good example from all three distances. In the surrounding city, as you glimpse the building from street corners and raised walkways, you see it in its totality: a set of dark glass blocks raised on thin Le Corbusier-style columns, which would by themselves be boring but

instead have hung between them a series of huge raised tropical gardens. Deep platforms between each block hold tall trees and rows of plants whose tendrils dangle down through the air. These unusual draping creepers seem to give the repetitive structure just the right amount of necessary visual complexity, and help to create a powerful sense of place.

Back in the 1960s, Prime Minister Lee Kuan Yew declared his intention to balance Singapore's urban environment with greenery, and began to turn it into 'a city in a garden'. Today, it's common to see ultra-modern towers in Singapore with gardens on their roofs or cut-out sections on high floors. But few do it as dramatically or as successfully as this.

Drawing closer to the street view, you realise that most of the building's interest has been concentrated at its lower floors. From the other side of a pedestrian crossing, your eyes are drawn upwards and then along the street. They track the rows of soldier-like columns that give pace and rhythm to all the lavish, teeming greenery. You also notice that the deep sections beneath the raised hotel-room blocks are not built out of straight lines, but ribbons of different tones that move in and out in unpredictable curves, playing with light and shade, and creating an effect that almost makes you feel like you're gazing at an ancient cliff face that's been worn away by thousands of years of ocean tides.

And just like a fractal, the closer you move to the hotel, the more interesting details reveal themselves. A water feature stretches the entire length of the building at two different heights, and underneath the surface of the water a floor of dark, flat pebbles gives a similar calming, contemplative feeling as a Japanese garden. Trees are arranged repetitively around this river-like structure, and a special pavement alongside the road is made up of different inexpensive coloured paving materials, with edges that move unpredictably in and out. Meanwhile, a glass roof protects you from the rain and the sun, and above that, the base of the upper floor is clearly visible and you realise that the undulating ribbons have unexpected deep ridges that give the light and shade yet another place to play and add even more interest.

After my visit, I learned that the Singapore planners had worked very closely with the architects to make the building special. This is a hotel that's generously extending its luxuries to everyone who passes by it, and not just to its guests. It's a building that cares deeply about the space it's taking up in its city, and is enthusiastic to share its wonder with everyone who encounters it, whether near or far, by foot or by bus. It's the precise opposite of the Pinnacle Hotel Harbourfront in Vancouver that I passed by at the start of my journey and that offered nothing

But you don't need tens of millions of dollars and a luxury hotel client to make buildings that are interesting from the three distances. On the busy North Circular Road, on the outskirts of London, a social housing project has been built that is just as successful as Singapore's Parkroyal Collection hotel.

Designed by Peter Barber Architects and commissioned by the Greater London Authority, Edgewood Mews is a dense complex of ninety-seven homes that looks from a distance like a medieval castle wall. This feels appropriate for its location. It's as if it's stoutly defending its inhabitants from the noisy and hostile road that runs alongside it.

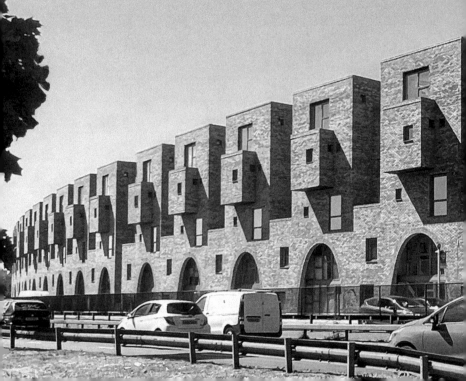

But rather than being built as the most basic box shape, its outline moves up and down in a way that's dramatic and interesting and tells you, even from far away, that this development is offering more than the minimum to the world.

As you draw closer towards the street view, Edgewood Mews becomes even more interesting. You realise that people are living inside these battlement walls. The wall ends aren't blocky and minimal but rounded towers with unusual rooflines. Oversized balconies jut out from the dwellings like drawbridges. The complex is actually made up of two 'walls' of connected buildings that have a path winding between them. The width of the path is perfect. It's neither so narrow that it seems spooky and forbidding, nor so wide that it feels alienating. The fact that it's curved creates a sense of curiosity that draws you in and invites you to explore, and the fact it's made of dark blocks instead of tarmac signals that this is a place for human feet rather than car tyres. You can see the path's success as a social space because, even though this development is still partly under construction when I visit, children are already happily playing outside.

At the door view, Edgewood Mews continues to offer new discoveries. On the ground floor, a series of tall and surprising – almost Gaudí-esque – arches create surprise and rhythm. The bricks that make up the outside surfaces of the development look old and reclaimed even though they might not be. There's a playful variety in the windows. Some pop out of the wall and others are slits, like those in a castle that a medieval archer might shoot arrows through. The doors and windows don't align with each other, instead making a jaunty pattern that's almost like looking at a musical score that's bouncing around. The steps leading up to each home twist around and up, so you feel like you're on a mini-adventure even when you're just going to your own front door.

There would have been immense pressure to save money on Edgewood Mews, and yet it has succeeded in being deeply human.

Playful brick on new building,
as if repaired

Unusually placed wall on
stairs appears insignificant,
but makes a great place
for a child to squeeze into

371

There are three crucial ways
we can shift our thinking if we
want our buildings to follow

THE
HUMANIZE
RULE:

A

ACCEPT THAT HOW USERS FEEL ABOUT A BUILDING IS A CRITICAL PART OF ITS FUNCTION.

B

**DESIGN BUILDINGS
WITH THE
HOPE AND EXPECTATION
THAT THEY'LL LAST
1,000 YEARS.**

C

**CONCENTRATE
A BUILDING'S
INTERESTING QUALITIES
AT THE
2-METRE
DOOR DISTANCE.**

EMOTION AS A FUNCTION

The Modernists believed that 'form follows function'. This meant that the outside appearance of a building should be the consequence of how it worked on the inside. If the building looked like anything more than its function, it was dishonest, embarrassing, even preposterous.

What was missing from their argument was that human emotion is a critical function.

Humans are driven by powerful emotions that are felt instantly and automatically. Every building we pass inspires feelings. On the most basic level, a building makes us feel good or it make us feel bad. It attracts or repels.

However well a home, office, shop or hospital works on the inside, if it repels its residents, workers, customers or patients from the outside, it's failing.

A fundamental part of a building's function is the emotions it inspires in everyone who experiences it. Designers should get more used to putting themselves in the shoes of both categories of their building's future users. This means imagining how their passers-by feel, and not just their occupants.

The medieval cathedral makers (and Le Corbusier at Ronchamp) were geniuses at understanding how buildings can inspire powerful emotions. When you walk into a cathedral, you're struck immediately by darkness and coolness and the echoes around the stonework. You hush your voice and look heavenwards towards the spectacular vaults and ceilings. Your breathing slows and you feel calmer and more meditative. The building deeply affects how you feel. The decisions of its designers who died centuries ago still manage to reach in and change you. They knew that emotion was a critically important function of their structures.

The best designers use emotion as a tool. The French
designer Philippe Starck is probably the king of
using emotion in objects such as chairs, door handles,
and his iconic lemon squeezer. These are ordinary
everyday items that in Starck's hands make us
feel something.

Likewise, the technologist and Apple co-founder Steve Jobs had an innate understanding of emotion as something that design could affect and play with. When he started out, he instinctively knew the public felt that computers were too complex, forbidding and inhuman. His genius was to transform the way we felt about electronics by making them more human. Jobs studied calligraphy as a young man. 'I learned about serif and sans serif typefaces,' he said, 'about varying the amount of space between different letter combinations, about what makes great typography great. It was beautiful, historical, artistically subtle in a way that science can't capture, and I found it fascinating...ten years later, when we were designing the first Macintosh computer, it all came back to me. And we designed it all into the Mac. It was the first computer with beautiful typography.'

Jobs's obsession with how his customers felt about Apple extended to the design of his stores, and even the packaging the products came in. A high-security room in Apple's headquarters contains many hundreds of prototype packages, with experts employed to test and refine them, making sure they inspire precisely the right kind of joy, impatience and excitement. 'Packaging can be theatre,' Jobs once said. 'It can create a story.'

Apple products haven't always beaten the competition in terms of technical innovation or sheer performance. But they have won consistently by understanding emotion as a primary function. This has helped the company to become worth $2 trillion.

Jobs drove Apple to success by striving to see the world through the eyes of his customers, and working out how to make them feel good. In his view, the people who bought his products weren't stupid or ignorant but could be trusted to respond positively to beauty and sophistication.

Building designers should be inspired by the faith Steve Jobs had in the public. We should stop the nonsensical mindset that says the public are ignorant and wrong. They can't be. Buildings that are loved by the public are rarely pulled down. It's ultimately up to them what gets demolished in the future and what gets protected. So the public should be the building designer's muse, who inspires and fascinates them. The public are the architect's most important audience, not other architects.

1,000-YEAR THINKING

ENTRY TO THE TRAITORS GATE

We should insist on a world in which building designers use a 1,000-year mindset.

New buildings must be designed to weather and flex with the natural movement of the ground, and get worn and dirty and be able to be easily repaired and reused. Structures designed with this mindset might not actually last for 1,000 years, but they're far more likely to be loved by the average passer-by and so resist future calls to have them knocked down.

As well as being boring, the buildings we demolish are often designed for just one use. For example, the ceilings in modern housing blocks tend to be set at their lowest allowable height in order to pile more flats on top of each other and maximise profits for the developer and landlord. This means that if the residential use is no longer right for the building, it's much harder to be used in a different way for something else. If these blocks were built with the intention that they were to be used and reused for the next 1,000 years, features such as ceiling heights would be made higher, as this allows for potential repurposing in the future.

THE TOWER OF LONDON WILL CELEBRATE ITS 1,000TH BIRTHDAY THIS CENTURY. IT'S BEEN A PRISON, A ROYAL MINT, A HOME FOR THE CROWN JEWELS, A VENUE FOR ART INSTALLATIONS AND A ZOO.

383

Building designers should always assume they're going to be a bit wrong about what their structure is ultimately for. This doesn't mean their buildings should be infinitely flexible, with moveable walls and a blandly inoffensive aesthetic. It's a matter of designing them with enough generosity that people will be both enthusiastic and able to reimagine and reuse them for generations to come.

And actually, many people think it's more fun to ambitiously adapt something old and interesting rather than create something new from scratch. My own studio has turned a South African grain silo into a museum, an English paper mill into a gin factory, and a pair of London warehouses into a shopping centre.

GRAIN SILO

MUSEUM

1,000-year buildings are those that can be adapted.

1,000-year buildings are those that most people don't want to see demolished.

Cultures like Japan have a long and inspiring history of 1,000-year thinking. They have aesthetic traditions such as *kintsugi*, in which gold is used to fix cracks in pottery.

It celebrates ageing, roughness and imperfection. When repairs to an object highlight its damage and turn it into something that looks different and even more interesting, this is 1,000-year thinking.

When my studio was given the challenge of designing the new London buses, we adopted a similar approach for the seats. We knew the fabric would have to survive the wear and tear of hundreds of thousands of backs, bottoms and grubby hands. Instead of picking a plain colour, we developed a pattern that our research said would best survive the onslaught of abrasion and dirt. This mindset of designing something to 'look good dirty' has stuck around in the culture of the studio and continues to inform our work.

PRIORITISE DOOR DISTANCE

This is the most important of the three distances, as it has the most emotional impact on passers-by. The human experience of any building is always going to be focused at the door distance. We the public spend most of our time on the ground, walking around and experiencing the world at eye level. We aren't in helicopters looking down, as people too often look down at architectural models.

Even if new buildings manage to succeed at the city and street distances, virtually all of them fail at the door distance. There are a few famous modern towers in London which are fantastic from a city distance but weak close up. When you're right beside them, they are boring. Building designers should do their most interesting and creative work at the door distance, where it will have the greatest impact. They should continually be imagining the emotional experiences of people walking past their buildings every day, year after year.

With every single step, how will their building make you feel?

See p. 494 for selected captions.

As modern buildings have become wider and wider, the prioritisation of door distance is more important than ever.

Historically, when human places were allowed to evolve naturally, they were on the human scale and full of interest. Streets in the old parts of cities such as Barcelona and Paris draw millions of visitors, because they're crammed with interesting human details at all three distances – but especially from the door distance. These places tend to have a more vertical emphasis, because the sites for buildings in the past used to be smaller. Narrower site plots next to each other always make streets that are more interesting and visually diverse, because you automatically get more opportunity for different buildings within a given street length. Conversely, if you look at the streets you find most boring, they're probably the ones that have the widest building plots and frontages. The problem with these wide buildings is that humans need to see changing details as they walk past. These enormous structures keep being built because architects are frequently instructed to create buildings that are the size of a city block or bigger. (I've been asked to do this many times too.) When building on such exaggerated scales – so removed from the size of human beings – it's vital that we compensate for all the unnatural bigness. We especially need to resist the easy lure of designing using repetitive horizontal lines – all those long flat windows and long flat floor slabs. Horizontal lines on buildings are extremely easy to draw when you're sitting in a design studio, but they work against the way humans perceive, which is to see along much more readily than to see up. Too much horizontality hogs our eyeline and creates deadening monotonous repetition. It quickly outstays its welcome by just going along and along and along some more.

ELEPHANTS

Whenever I talk to people about humanizing buildings, the same points tend to come up. Some wonder if the only way to achieve what we want is to go back to the past.

N THE ROOM

Others worry it means smothering buildings in decorations, like Christmas trees. But most commonly they're convinced the mission is not realistically possible with modern materials or budgets.

Is DECORATION THE ANSWER?

GO BACK
TO THE PAST?

SHOULD WE COPY OLD BUILDINGS?

JAPAN

YEMEN

When people discuss their feelings about buildings, the conversation often descends into a predictable, simplistic argument – with those who prefer the old styles on one side and those who prefer the new styles on the other.

I believe it's possible to unite these opposing camps by looking at the issue a little differently.

One thing people love about older buildings is their sense of place.

AUSTRALIA

NIGERIA

Humans have always looked at their buildings to discover who they are.

These houses in Japan, Yemen, Australia and Nigeria have a sense of their cultures built into them. They have a powerful sense of place.

Some of the UK's most popular buildings are ones that reflect the nation's visual culture. London's Tower Bridge was designed in a sixteenth-century Gothic style but it's actually a huge piece of Victorian mechanical engineering, and was completed in 1896. It was built with a 1,000-year mindset. It's ludicrous but beloved. Nobody is clamouring to have Tower Bridge torn down – despite its apparent 'dishonesty', as the Modernists would say.

And yet there's a powerful movement inside the world of architecture against new buildings that adopt older styles. They get called 'derivative' and 'insincere' and 'pastiche' and 'inauthentic'.

FRANCE: BUILT 2006

Opposite: Place de Toscane, Marne-la-Vallée. Pier Carlo Bontempi in association with Dominique Hertenberger

Right: One Nimman, Chiang Mai. Ong-ard Architects

In the US, American Colonial, Prairie and Googie styles remain popular. They still like the Federation style in Australia and the Chalet style in Switzerland. In the UK it's Edwardian, Georgian, Victorian, and Arts and Crafts. They're not the kind of buildings I make, but I recognise they're part of who we are as a nation, like Cheddar cheese and Charles Dickens. Whether it's in Britain, Japan or Mauritania, I don't believe a building that reflects its historic culture is automatically bad. If these buildings make the people who use them feel good, then why should we look down our noses at them? When we see a recreated Japanese ryokan in Tokyo, we don't scream 'derivative' here in the UK. The new buildings of the last century have done untold times more damage to our cities and towns than so-called derivative buildings from the same period.

I don't think we in the architectural profession should have a kind of god complex that demands that people must only invent building styles from scratch. We shouldn't be afraid of honouring our culture and the people who built our past, as long as we do it wholeheartedly.

But neither should we be afraid of designing buildings that look like the future.

Above: Richmond Riverside, London. Quinlan Terry

Opposite: Harold Washington Library Center, Chicago. Hammond, Beeby and Babka

402

USA
BUILT 1991

Here in Britain, you sometimes hear it said that the public don't like anything new – that, if it was left up to them, they'd reject anything modern and just want the world filled with Georgian-style houses and Tower Bridges. But these assumptions (often, I suspect, made in bitterness over Modernist designs being rejected) underestimate the diversity of people's interests and tastes.

As we've already discovered, the top ten most-loved buildings in the world include Burj Khalifa, Hallgrímskirkja and The Shard.

Burj Khalifa (shown here) doesn't reflect much about the history of its place in the desert of Dubai. It's popular because it's interesting enough from a city distance to create its own sense of place. The Parkroyal Collection hotel in Singapore also doesn't reflect much about the history of its place. It succeeds because it's interesting enough from all three distances to create its own sense of place.

Many of the great building designers in history have pulled off a similar trick. Georges-Eugène Haussmann's buildings in Paris are often assumed to reflect an essential Parisian sense of place, but in fact they created it. They were a derivative version of a classical style built with a wholehearted conviction.

What do the old and new human buildings have in common? Necessary visual complexity.

The London houses designed by Thomas Cubitt in nineteenth-century London have necessary visual complexity. These buildings might not be to your taste. To some they appear pompous and fusty. But they have three-dimensionality and simple decorative details and sometimes even curves.

The Pompidou Centre, built in Paris in the 1970s, also has necessary visual complexity. Again, this building might not be to your taste: to some it appears harshly industrial and chaotic. But when you look at it, you keep seeing more and more details.

The Pompidou Centre has necessary visual complexity.

Thomas Cubitt's houses have necessary
visual complexity.

They are human.

IS DECORATION
THE ANSWER?

THE 'D' WORD

An all-too-easy way to add necessary visual complexity
is by using decoration. But complexity doesn't need
to be a layer that's added onto a building like 'lipstick
on a gorilla'. In my work with my studio, we don't
want to make buildings that are decorat*ed*. Instead,
we have a mindset of taking what we need to build
anyway, and trying to make it sufficiently complex.
You could say this means being decorat*ive* rather
than decorat*ed*. Wherever possible, complexity isn't
mindlessly added onto the surface of the building
but expressed in the structure itself. Interestingness
can be generated by how you frame a window or door,
in how you join surfaces together, and by showing
rather than hiding the craft that went into it. We
don't strive to eliminate details on the outsides of
buildings, but rather to amplify and augment them.

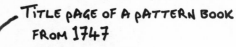
TITLE PAGE OF A PATTERN BOOK FROM 1747

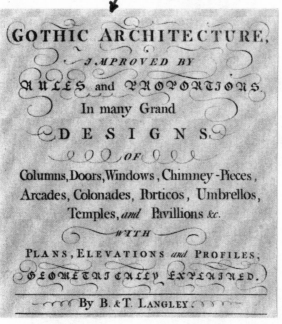

GOTHIC ARCHITECTURE,
IMPROVED BY
RULES and PROPORTIONS.
In many Grand
DESIGNS
OF
Columns, Doors, Windows, Chimney-Pieces,
Arcades, Colonades, Porticos, Umbrellos,
Temples, *and* Pavillions &c.
WITH
PLANS, ELEVATIONS *and* PROFILES,
GEOMETRICALLY EXPLAINED.
By B. & T. LANGLEY.

In Victorian and Georgian Britain, a system existed that helped designers easily create interesting buildings. Pattern books were catalogues of drawings of pre-designed doors, windows, columns, mouldings, cornices, pediments and gargoyles. They contained everything you'd need to create many kinds of buildings, as the elements could be combined in different configurations and proportions. These books provided building designers with a ready-made system of visual complexity which meant they weren't starting every new project from scratch.

Door Ironwork

Windows

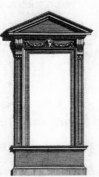
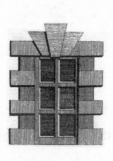

Doors

Railings

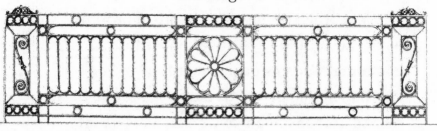

 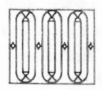 

Windows

Doors

The Modernists threw the culture of pattern books away, and all the usefulness they contained. Today's designers often end up creating boring buildings because they've been robbed of the wisdom and convenience that the system of pattern-book thinking could give them. Could we conceive of a new era of pattern books compiled for makers of human buildings that don't slavishly copy the designs of the past?

2026 EDITION

A COLLECTION OF DESIGNS IN ARCHITECTURE

WINDOWS
DOORS
BALCONIES
RAILINGS

LIGHTING
ELEVATORS
CLADDING
COLUMNS

of humanising design ideas for doors, windows ... and more

TOO
EXPENSIVE?

THE
HUMAN PREMIUM

It's undoubtedly true that making human buildings
is harder than making boring ones. Achieving
necessary visual complexity was much easier for
the designers of the past because complexity was
already naturally present in the ingredients of their
buildings. When making new structures, we'll always
be nudged towards the most inexpensive and efficient
surfacing materials such as glass, thin aluminium
sheeting and silicone sealant. These modern,
mass-produced materials typically have a sterile
appearance. They're bland and empty and make
a poor canvas for time to write its message.

As the materials themselves are so characterless,
we need to work harder to amplify character and the
potential for interestingness. If we're going to use

aluminium, can we make panels that are interestingly un-flat? If we're going to use mass-produced bricks, can we insist they're not all of a uniform tone or colour? Can we put them together to create three-dimensional patterns that engage the eye, and grow more visually complex with the decades-long onslaught of weather and dirt? Or maybe we could do something interesting with the mortar instead? And if we're not going to use older types of materials such as brick, which automatically look better as they get older, whatever we replace them with needs to do the same job. But the worry is that human materials and techniques cost too much.

Tight budgets are an inevitability. But we can't let ourselves use them as an excuse to make yet more boring buildings. People sometimes imagine that in my own studio we spend our time dreaming up exciting ideas and then clients immediately say yes and pay for whatever we want. This is not true, of course. Most of our design time is spent going round and round, redesigning and redesigning and trying to be as resourceful and focused and ingenious as possible with the limited amount of money we've been given.

When we finished the UK Pavilion for the 2010 World
Expo in Shanghai, an architect from another country
came in and remarked on how lucky I was because he

didn't get the budget that we had. But I'd been told that in reality he'd had almost twice our financial resources.

When my studio was commissioned to make The Hive, a complex of classrooms at Singapore's Nanyang Technological University, we were faced with tight financial constraints.

Sometimes the answer was to simply and literally go the extra mile. We were desperate to make the paving around the building interesting, but could only afford extremely cheap and boring clay tiles. So one day a member of my team went out into the city and walked for many hours, from one local building merchant to the next, asking: 'Do you have any stone that's the same price as tiles? Is there anything you can give me?'

Eventually he found someone who could supply a leftover job lot of extraordinary quartzite stones that had a silvery quality that's almost like fish skin.

At other times we had to be imaginative with our processes. The outside of The Hive is made up of 1,000 curved concrete panels made in neighbouring Malaysia. Even though we could only afford one mould to make them all in, we were determined that each panel should look different. To achieve this, we put a special chemical gel inside the mould that stopped the surface of the cement from setting, so that when you washed it back you were left with a wonderful rough stony texture visible beneath. We put the gel in a different place on every panel to create the maximum complexity and variety. We also designed the mould so that we could bend it to a different radius every time we used it, slightly changing the angle of the curves, and placed pieces of rubber at various places along its interior wall. These changes added much more variety and an unpredictable three-dimensionality. When I first saw the results, the perfectionist in me freaked out and thought, 'What are we doing? This isn't perfect enough.' But when I saw them being put together, I realised it was their imperfections that made them precious. If we'd only had perfect panel after perfect panel, it would have added up to perfect boredom.

Aside from the building's huge oval rooms piled on top of one another, much of the wall space of The Hive is made up of solid structural concrete walls embedded with designs based on 700 ink drawings by the artist Sara Fanelli. These designs often repeat, but are so complex and carefully arranged that it's unlikely any passer-by would notice. We could only afford the cheapest concrete, whose surface is filled with endless imperfections of bubbles and stones. But Fanelli's gorgeous designs distract the eye, tricking it into not noticing how rough the concrete really is. The final building is utterly raw, but feels warm and interesting and friendly and didn't cost much more than a similarly sized car park.

It did cost a bit more. It wasn't much. But if we're serious about re-humanizing our world, we have to talk about that 'bit' and accept that it matters. We have to change how we think. Whether we're a city planner, a property developer, a politician, a critic, an educator, or an ordinary citizen who refuses to allow their world and the world of their children to be smothered by deadening buildings, we must demand from each other the extra effort and budget that human buildings take.

Re-humanization means nothing less than a shift in values.

Does this sound impossible? It shouldn't. Our shared values are constantly in flux: we're not the same people today as we were 100 years ago. When I was little and brought dried bananas into school, I was considered a freak (and my mum ate macrobiotic food and my father wore Birkenstock sandals fifteen years before Kate Moss made them fashionable). Now all of this has changed.

We're not the same people as we were even half a generation ago. On a massive range of issues – everything from race to gender to our ideas about sustainability and the environment – we have evolved. We smoke less, use seatbelts more, and a greater number of us eat a vegan diet. Following outrage over the Port Arthur massacre in Australia in 1996, legislation and public attitudes towards guns changed radically – with the result that fewer Australians than ever are killed with firearms. And in the UK there's been a major shift in values over the last couple of decades in how we think about food. In 2005 we banned the industrialised food product Turkey Twizzlers from school meals following a campaign by the television cook Jamie Oliver.

We decided cheapness wasn't the most
important value.

We decided the food our children eat shouldn't
taste like efficiency.

It's time we insist that our buildings are 'nutritious'
too, and nourish us as we encounter them.

We should confidently reject the tired old argument
that property developers can't be expected to make
human places because they're hard-nosed capitalists
with a bottom line to worry about.

150 years ago, property developers were also hard-nosed capitalists with a bottom line to worry about. They wanted profit too. But they made the effort of using curves, eaves, mouldings, cornice work and stained glass above their front doors. If they could do it at scale when average income and quality of life was so much lower, why can't we?

It's also not true that interesting buildings were cheaper to build back then. As the US architect Michael Benedikt writes:

'The pre-World War II buildings that people prize today – buildings with high ceilings, operable windows, well-defined rooms, clarifying mouldings, solid walls and pleasing decoration, the ones we sigh we can no longer build today "because they would cost too much" – were not cheaper to build back then. Indeed, they were relatively more expensive to build back then and they absorbed proportionately more of our then-wealth, time and income.'

Society has chosen to spend less on each individual building we now build. It's not surprising they aren't emotionally nutritious enough.

And then comes the next excuse: but we're in a time of crisis today! Look at all the things that are going wrong. Human buildings are a low priority in the face of all this urgency.

We must counter the endlessly delaying mindset that always says the sky is falling on our heads and therefore we can't afford to make good buildings. When will the time come when there's no crisis to justify cheapness?

It's true that we're going through a terrible climate crisis, which matters immensely. But the simultaneous reality is we're richer than we've ever been at any point in history. We also spend more money on building than at any point in history. The amount we threw at construction globally grew from $9.5 trillion in 2014 to $11.4 trillion in 2019.

We could afford to make good, simple, human buildings

We could afford to make good, simple, human buildings

We could afford to make good, simple, human buildings

We could afford to make good, simple, human buildings

n the year **1723.**

n the year **723.**

n the year **23.**

n the year **3.**

Every other generation of humans managed to do it, up until the early decades of the twentieth century. There is no doubt that we can do it today.

But how do we figure out how much is the right amount extra to spend?

One technique we've used in my studio is to create two options to discuss with a client. The first represents the most affordable way to complete their project so it fulfils its basic functions and meets necessary regulations. This minimum version is invariably non-human but establishes a base. We then study truly human versions that cost perhaps 5–10 per cent more than the base solution. From there we begin deep and honest discussions with the client about the costs and benefits, without seeming naive about money. These are the most interesting conversations.

And remember that even with their extra initial expense, human buildings are likely to end up being far cheaper in the long run because there's less chance they'll be demolished, avoiding the need for yet more expensive new buildings. The global waste cost from the construction industry is projected to reach $34.4 billion annually by 2026. In the US, around 90 per cent of this waste is from demolition.

That's a lot of money wasted on buildings that aren't loved enough to be saved. By re-humanizing the world, we can save billions of dollars and dramatically reduce the amount of carbon that's released into the atmosphere as a result of demolition.

As an industry, we've started to become used to the idea of a 'green premium' that ensures our buildings are more sustainable by applying an accepted ecological standard. A growing number of clients for new buildings accept this premium. Sometimes they do more than accept it – they're proud of it. The green premium reflects a broad societal shift in values over recent decades towards prioritising the protection of our planet. But to be truly sustainable, this is not the full picture.

It's time to insist on a . . .

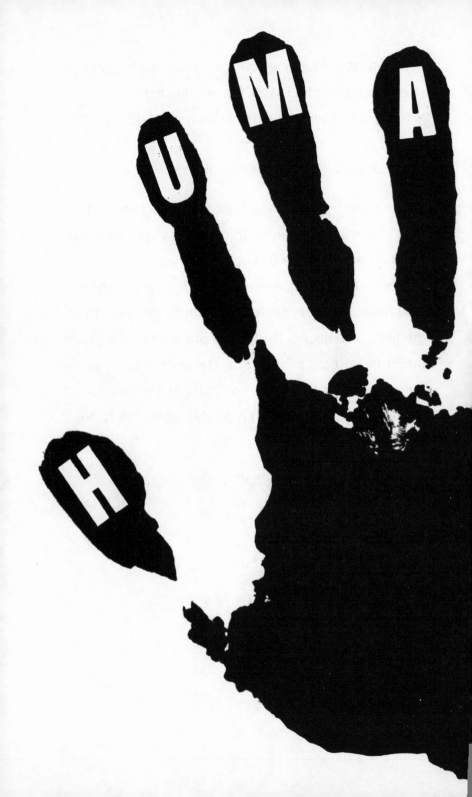

PREMIUM

CHANGING

A new movement to humanize the world can't just
rely on shifts in our thinking. Ending the blandemic
and dismantling the cult of Modernist architecture
is going to require a revolution in the way the
construction industry and the ordinary passer-by
act. Over the three decades I've been trying to build

WHAT WE DO

human buildings, I've been lucky enough to have had amazing conversations with many inspiring people about how to make meaningful change. On the following pages are some ideas for what we might do to build a more human world.

Rethink the Profession of Architecture

Back in the nineteenth century, when architecture was being professionalised and protected, a historic error was made.

In 1892, a short book was published filled with the passionate voices of building designers who were anxious about the consequences of this change. *Architecture, a Profession or an Art: Thirteen Short Essays on the Qualifications and Training of Architects* is fascinating in the predictions made by its authors. In the introduction, Thomas Graham Jackson, the designer of Oxford's much-loved Bridge of Sighs, argues that: 'The architect suffers at present through his isolation from the sister arts of painting and sculpture. To tighten the bonds of professionalism would be to shut him off from them entirely and to smother what little of the artist is left in him . . . If architecture is ever to live again amongst us, the professional idea must disappear.'

In the same pages, the Gothic architect George Frederick Bodley writes: 'What we are protesting against is the attempt to make the profession of architecture a close and certified calling, on the strength of examinations that can be no true test of artistic capability. What we claim for it is the high freedom of an art that shall stand as a queen unfettered . . .'

The worries and predictions of these men have been proven right again and again over the last century. Since their book was published, the role of the 'architect' has indeed become over-professionalised and removed from the world of true artists.

As well as this, the profession has become accessible only to people who possess the hugely significant amount of time and resources that you need to gain entry. Even in the suffocatingly class-bound nineteenth century, it was possible for working-class men like Gustave Eiffel and Joseph Paxton to work their way up to construct two of the most beloved structures in their countries (the Eiffel Tower and the Crystal Palace respectively), and to embody, writes historian Adam Sharr, 'the image of self-made practical people that just got on with things, in opposition to scholarly gentleman architects'.

Can we repair some of the damage that's been done by over-professionalisation – by rethinking what an architect is, how they're trained and how architecture itself is practised?

When we encountered the Modernists, I observed that many of our most influential architects viewed themselves as artists. Even Le Corbusier, the paradoxical God of Boring himself, believed that 'architecture is the art above all others'.

You might assume that I view such thinking as naive, arrogant or delusional.

I don't.

I do not believe the problem is that architects see themselves as artists. On the contrary, I believe that architects are indeed responsible for making the biggest artistic objects in the world. The real problem is that what they do most of the time cannot be called 'art' at all. They fool themselves into believing they're being artistic when in fact they've let themselves be constrained by conventional thinking. Meanwhile, the resistance to non-architects getting chances to make significant buildings is real.

About twenty-five years ago, a major competition was announced to design a contemporary art gallery. I wanted to enter this competition but because the entry requirements said you had to be a qualified architect, I wasn't able to enter. A few years later, I went to a talk in London by the director and lead judge. They told the audience that their favourite-ever art gallery was one in Germany that had been designed by an artist rather than an architect. I raised my hand and asked, 'How come your favourite art museum is designed by an artist, and yet you made your own competition impossible for an artist to enter?'

They replied, 'Well, actually there was a collaborating artist working with the winning architect.' But despite being familiar with the finished building, I'd never heard of this artist's involvement. This showed how little their contribution was valued.

I left that talk feeling unsatisfied with what I'd heard. But it did give me a glimpse of a possible future in which artistic thinking would be allowed to once again flourish in the art of architecture.

UNLEASH

THE ARTISTS

One reason why architects might not be thinking so artistically anymore is that the job itself has become enormously complex. Over the last 100 years, the legal, political and regulatory aspects of building have been massively expanded. The technologies and options involved in making a building have multiplied exponentially. To be artistic, as well as safe, as well as sustainable, as well as a political spokesperson, as well as a salesperson, as well as a leader of disparate teams, is an impossible job.

The romantic vision of the masterful leader who's in charge of everything from the creation of an inspiring scheme to doing all the drawings and management and costings and navigating regulations and leading builders is ridiculous. I know I certainly can't do all this.

We should find ways of getting a more diverse group of people to help share the load and offer different sensibilities. Entry into the profession could be far more inclusive: qualifications that take up to seven years are impossible for most people to even contemplate unless they come from a significantly resourced background and are of a certain age.

There must be more ways to open up the profession and unlock the stranglehold of academia and professionalisation. Perhaps we can imagine shorter, less expensive courses that focus more on making and the creative and emotional aspects of building design. This would encourage social mobility into the profession, and perhaps even more importantly bring a greater diversity of backgrounds, perspectives and ideas.

Another way to unshackle the profession is by collaborating more with other kinds of creative people. Architects such as Gaudí worked with many artists who didn't just make the doorknobs or light fixtures but also had a profound holistic impact on his projects. There's a huge untapped potential for firms to collaborate in extraordinary ways with high-profile figures from other disciplines. Can you imagine what a Wes Anderson office block, a Björk parliament building, a George R. R. Martin hotel or a development of 800 affordable homes by Banksy would look and feel like? I would love to work alongside artists like these to do something useful and meaningful.

I've also had the chance to work on projects with great architects such as Foster + Partners, BIG and Lina Ghotmeh as partners designing buildings together. While my team and I are very different from them, and bring different thoughts and talents to a collaboration, we've always worked under an agreement that all credit (and blame) is shared equally. I love that we'll never tell anybody where a particular idea came from. This allows us to worry less about silly ego stuff and instead collaborate with a true spirit of adventure.

HUMANIZE

But collaboration alone isn't going to be enough to dismantle the cult of boring. We also need to address the industry's self-perpetuating cycle of cult thinking. The current educational model of older masters indoctrinating generations of impressionable young people could be replaced with methods that have already proven successful in the world of computer coding. Organisations like École 42 in France and 01 Founders in the UK have been revolutionising the way creativity is nurtured, by pioneering teacher-less 'peer-to-peer learning'. This unusual new technique empowers students to guide each other and work out their own solutions, rather than having them dictated by lecturers.

WOT, NO TEACHERS?

EDUCATION

For the world of architecture, I could imagine developing a self-directed learning programme that encourages students to look at the world with their feelings as well as their intellect. 'Crits' would happen in a hierarchy-free environment. The thrilling potential of this would be the creation of a new wave of talented and relatively baggage-free practitioners. It's incredibly exciting to imagine the aesthetic diversity that could be unleashed in place of the dull conformity we still see too much of today.

It's also always seemed surprising to me that, in the British education system, trainee architects have hardly any engagement with city planners. Learning how to look through the eyes of a planner should be an essential part of the syllabus, and by extension another way of seeing through the eyes of the public.

Could we also improve the way planners themselves are educated? Perhaps they could be trained in the principles of humanized building and taught to focus more on the human experience than the nitty-gritty of policy? Surely they should be encouraged to be constantly challenging the construction industry with questions such as: How is this project human? How will it make people feel? Is emotion a primary function? Does it have the necessary visual complexity from door distance? Where is the 1,000-year thinking?

Finally, wouldn't it be brilliant if we could train more makers? As the Modernist movement's demand for specialist workers such as carvers, lead-workers, glassmakers and plasterers died out, so too did the professions. 150 years ago, there would have been millions of highly skilled craftspeople on the planet ready to contribute to the task of making interesting buildings.

We mustn't be overly romantic about historic forms of craft, however. Making new interesting buildings doesn't necessarily mean harking back to old-fashioned materials and processes.

3D PRINTING A WALL:
A MOVING NOZZLE SQUEEZES OUT LAYERS OF CONCRETE LIKE TOOTHPASTE.

There are lots of amazing new ways of creating three-dimensional forms and visual complexity – including techniques like laser-cutting, computer-controlled machining of materials and 3D printing of a building's walls. Just imagine what innovations Gaudí and Haussmann would have created if they'd had access to these new making techniques – and what a new generation of creatives could do if they were educated in human design.

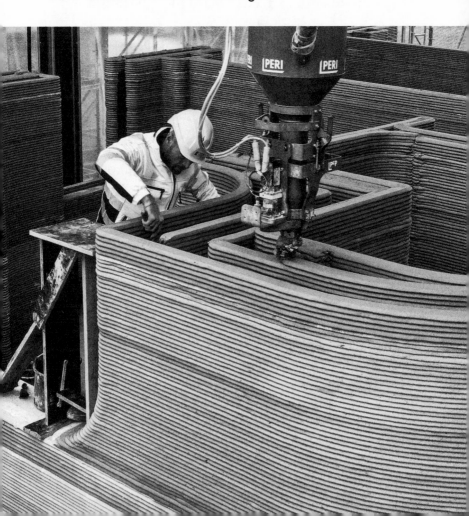

HUMANIZE

Planning processes are often hostile to the public.
In the UK we're still tying planning notices full of tiny
jargon-filled writing to lamp posts. And even though
drawings of proposed buildings can be found online,
they remain hard to access, hard to understand and
hard to comment on. This process acts as a filter.
It reduces the presence of the ordinary interested
passer-by, and leaves mostly the angry, the determined
and the bloody-minded, who can all too easily be
dismissed as cranks and NIMBYs.*

Other countries have more twenty-first-century
approaches. In Canada I've seen colour images
on a street noticeboard that show the proposed
development, its footprint on a map, a QR code that
leads to a detailed virtual-reality model, and details
about how to leave comments and ask questions.

One way for planning applications to really connect
with people – and even be interesting and under-
standable to children – would be for them to also
be submitted in the world-building video game

* NIMBY: NOT IN MY BACK YARD

PLANNING

Minecraft. This hugely popular game is the virtual equivalent of Lego, and could be an easy way to model buildings that allows anyone to experience them before they're built.

Minecraft is already being used collaboratively by communities to reimagine public places and build togetherness.

The project Block by Block has helped groups in eastern Beirut to design and build a vacant public space in Bourj Hammoud, creating a place to gather, perform and play.

BUILDINGS AND LANDSCAPE MODELLED ENTIRELY IN MINECRAFT BY COMMUNITY MEMBERS

Wherever we are in the world, we need systems that invite the public in and that value them as the central client of all new public-facing buildings.

HUMANIZE

Today's regulatory system too often incentivises
a risk-averse boringness. But it is possible to have
regulations that encourage qualities such as three-
dimensionality. A lot of buildings in Hong Kong have
visual complexity, as a direct result of a government
initiative from a number of years ago that encouraged
bay windows. For a while, developers in the city
were told that they could increase the area they were
allowed to build inside their new residential towers,
by putting bay windows that stuck out as lumps on
the outsides. An apartment with bay windows was
desirable for the developers because they could
charge higher amounts for the enlarged area. But
more importantly, the towers that got built as a
result were no longer flat and smooth but much more
three-dimensional – and therefore more interesting
for everyone passing by.

When I was walking the streets of Barcelona, I also
noticed how much variety was generated by all the
sculptural balconies and even whole rooms that had
been allowed to stick out over the pavements.

REGULATIONS

As I walked along, there was a continual cascade of interest flowing over my head as building after building jutted out into the space above. As I looked down the street, it seemed so alive and full of personality. Could we allow property developers and architects to create balconies and rooms that overhang pavements, on the strict condition that they are interesting and non-continuous and that they add extra visual complexity? Property developers would get more space to sell, and the rest of us would get a more interesting world to live in.

A humanized set of regulations, unique to each city, could make it harder to make boringness and easier to make humanness.

It would incentivise developers to de-boring their buildings. It would be a win-win.

453

ARCHITECTURAL CENTRES

Places that are open, welcoming, fascinating and free to enter are critical if we want to engage passers-by. I realised I wanted to be a designer when my father took me to The Design Centre, located in the busy West End of London. If it hadn't existed, I don't know whether I would have ended up becoming a designer. All through my teenage years, I kept returning. But in 1998, that public face was shut down. How many potential designers has the UK lost since then because The Design Centre no longer exists?

Imagine if each country had a national architecture centre that was as exciting and accessible as The Design Centre once was. What if these centres were in all our major cities? Not only could we inspire a new, diverse generation of building designers, they could be places where plans for developments are shared and communities come together and feel invited to contribute.

FOR EVERYONE

Currently, the United Kingdom's symbolic centre of architectural excellence is the Royal Institute of British Architects. It's one of the best and most important architectural bodies in the world. And yet the design of its headquarters is forbidding and intimidating. It signals that the profession it represents is insufficiently interested in the true feelings of the public. How can the world's town and city centres have organisations like RIBA, but more visible and accessible to teenagers – like The Design Centre was for me?

Signing Buildings

One afternoon, a professional I know surprised me with his unusual frankness when he openly told me, 'I've built some terrible buildings during my career.' This admission made it immediately clear that we have a problem of too much anonymity in the industry these days. If we're going to create buildings, the people who put them up should be easily identifiable now. Instead of staying in the shadows, the designers, developers, councillors and even the heads of planning committees responsible for the construction of our world should be proudly named at eye level on the outsides of their projects.

Why would anyone involved in the process of building buildings be against this? Why wouldn't you be proud? Why wouldn't you want to sign your canvas?

HUMANIZE AWARDS

We need awards and accolades for new buildings that are led by the ordinary passer-by and not by the architectural profession and construction industry. We must stop celebrating the act of giving the public what they don't want. The weight of a jury panel should always be largely non-professional.

HUMANIZE

I already know what certain writers at certain
newspapers and magazines are going to say about
this book. There will be articles written by people
I could name right now, and comments on them
made by professionals. People I know I'll never be
able to convince.

So I realise what I'm about to say might sound like
pre-emptive sour grapes. But I promise this isn't
personal. I really believe it.

We need architecture critics who are more interested
in public feelings. It's easy to detect a general view
among some of our most celebrated commentators
that if a building is popular with ordinary people then
it's somehow trashy and embarrassing.

We need critics to stop talking so much about 'subtlety'
and 'simplicity', 'understatement', 'thoughtfulness',
'clean lines' and 'rigour', and instead take the human
factor seriously and notice when designers fail to
incorporate this. A few years ago, some computer
images of a major London project I was involved

ARCHITECTURAL CRITICISM

with were released earlier than I'd wanted. I knew that our work at the door distance wasn't good enough yet. But none of the main critics commented on this, focusing instead on the private roof garden and the wall cladding that was going to be high above the heads of passers-by. These were the least important parts to the millions of people who'd walk past it on the street.

If critics really want to improve the world, we need them to consider 99 per cent of buildings – the new-build tower blocks in regional towns; the sprawling housing estates on their outskirts – and not just the special 1 per cent in Sydney or Berlin or New York or Cape Town or Seoul. At the moment, they seem to spend 99 per cent of their time talking about this special 1 per cent of buildings, whose designers have tried especially hard anyway.

Most of all, we need critics who are fascinated to explore how buildings impact the emotions and lives of the millions of passers-by.

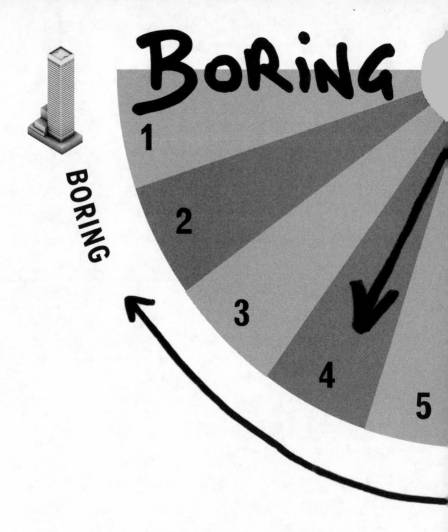

BORING

BORING

1

2

3

4

5

Another way to assess the presence of boring
(if it isn't already completely obvious) is by asking
yourself how flat, plain, straight or monotonous it is.
My studio has developed the Boringometer –
a customised software tool that lets professionals
measure the visual complexity of a building's design
from the point of view of the passer-by.

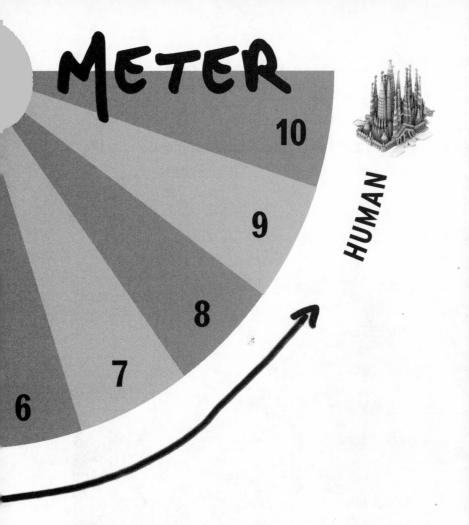

METER

10

9

8

7

6

HUMAN

A complex building, such as La Sagrada Família in Barcelona, scores 9/10. All the ordinary office buildings we've tested, score 1/10.

The Boringometer analyses the front of a building, measuring different types of complexity. It helps designers, clients and planners to discover just how visually engaging a new building might be for the people who will walk past it each day.

It's a bit like a digital version of a massive pin-art toy, pressed onto the front of a building.

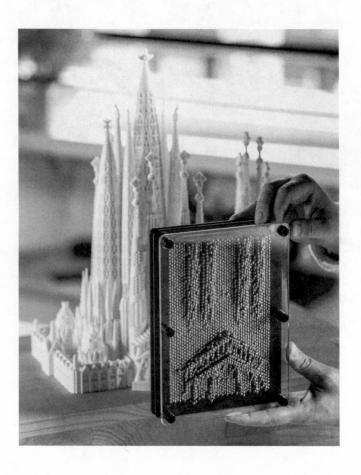

The diagram below shows how the Boringometer reads the humanized qualities of Casa Milà in Barcelona. 'Detail' is a reading of how a building's surface shifts and changes close-up. 'Massing' assesses the larger forms of the building such as the big elements that push in and stick out. 'Variation' combines these two readings to give a measurement of overall complexity.

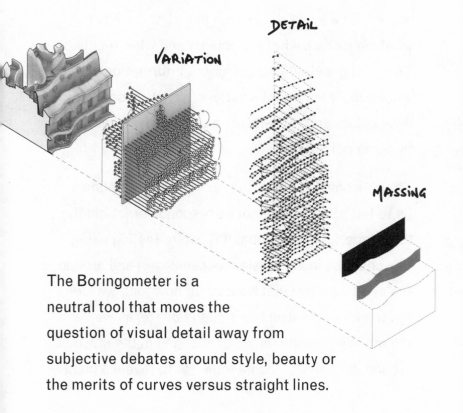

How THE BoRiNG-o-METER ANALySES CASA MiLÀ

VARiATioN

DETAiL

MASSiNG

The Boringometer is a neutral tool that moves the question of visual detail away from subjective debates around style, beauty or the merits of curves versus straight lines.

Whether or not a structure has sufficient complexity can now be more objectively assessed using the Boringometer's exact computer-calculated metric. We need to move towards a time in which cities mandate that any new development meets a minimum complexity score or ask its designers to give a reasonable justification for not doing so.

Many other powerful digital tools are rapidly becoming available that will allow building designers to understand people's experiences of buildings in a scientific way – how we use an existing place, how we act, what we look at, what attracts us and what repels us. They will give building designers information about what people want that's derived from thousands of data points and is therefore as close as we can get to being objective.

There is now also amazing technology that allows us to tell how each one of us responds emotionally to a place. Humans signal how we're feeling using tiny changes in expression, especially in and around the eyes. Exactly what we look at, how long we look for, the extent to which our pupils dilate, as well as the minutely subtle dance of changes in the muscles around our eyes, all come together to reveal a huge amount about how we feel when we experience a building. Think of the fleeting flick of the eyes at a particular detail. Or an unwitting frown, a raising of eyebrows, or a squint of anxiety. These tell us so much about what's going on in the minds, and hearts, of others. Combine this with smartwatches and fitness trackers that read fluctuations in heart rate, body temperature and stress response, and building designers will gain inarguable evidence that shows the extent to which any structure is human (or boring). It will even be possible to test the humanness of any new development as it's still being imagined, by feeding architectural plans into the virtual world and using headsets to crowdsource the responses of thousands, at scale.

New analytical tools such as these will only add to the mountain of evidence we already have that the desire for interestingness is part of human nature – and that human buildings aren't anti-Modernist but are actually more rational than the works of the old Modernists.

Technological advances such as these make me optimistic. The outlook is far from hopeless. As well as new analytical tools, there are also amazing new design tools such as the artificial intelligence platforms DALL-E, Stable Diffusion and Midjourney, which can help create unexpectedly interesting designs in a matter of seconds.

In colleges, there's a new generation of purpose-driven students – and teachers – determined to make real change. Joshua Vermillion, Professor of Architecture at the University of Nevada, uses AI to design buildings that are unexpected and interesting and is encouraging his students to do the same.

In the design profession, there are people doing fantastic human work like the architect Peter Barber, whose Edgewood Mews social housing project I visited.

And leaders of places like Singapore and Melbourne are beginning to speak about the qualities that make their city 'lovable'.

AI-GENERATED DESIGNS
BY JOSHUA VERMILLION

IT'S TIME TO SHOUT

There is a catastrophe unfolding that's affecting you and everyone you love. It has been happening for 100 years and counting. But it's a slow and stealthy process. You don't open your window one day, and where there was an interesting street see a grim Modernist plaza.

It all just happens in the background.

The hoarding screens are put up.

The demolition ball comes down.

Then come the cranes.

Then the mind-numbing boredom.

This activity tries to hide itself. But it's being done to you, just as a broken nose is done to you.

The continuation of the blandemic relies on the illusion that people are powerless.

We need to fearlessly demand interestingness in our places. We need to rebel against the Turkey Twizzlerification of our streets, towns and cities, and make buildings that nourish our senses.

Stop telling yourself this is a problem for later.

We've been forced to live through a lost century of harmful architecture.

It's made us more stressed, more angry, more scared, more divided – it's sickened our minds and sickened our planet.

By 2050, two out of every three of us will live in a town or city. We're going to have to build many thousands more homes, schools and hospitals.

We must no longer tolerate the putting up of boring buildings.

Human beings deserve human places.

Today, we're all the beneficiaries of the generous gifts past generations have given us. When we flock to see the beautiful buildings of Kyoto, Barcelona, Moscow, Prague, Marrakech and Luang Prabang, it's largely to see the works of designers who lived and worked before the cult of Modernism took over. Some of us are lucky enough to live in houses and apartment blocks that were built by these long-dead men and women. What gifts have our generation and the generation just past built for the citizens of the future? What places have we made that twenty-second-century tourists will spend time and money travelling across the planet just to see? The great majority of everyday buildings were once interesting. How many are today? Two per cent? One? We've acted shamefully, covering our towns and cities in unloved and unlovable buildings.

Boring buildings aren't just a curse on the visual landscape. They're a curse on our mental health. They make us stressed and anxious and scared. They're a curse on joy. They make us unhappy. They're a curse on fairness. The less privileged people are, the more their lives are blighted by boring. They're a curse on our planet. They're much more likely to be demolished. The destruction of the natural environment is the most urgent problem facing us today. Whilst the media focus on plastic straws, supermarket carrier bags and air travel, greater damage is being done by our addiction to knocking down unloved buildings and – far too often – replacing them with buildings that will be no more loved. The construction industry is responsible for five times more carbon emissions than aviation. It's a scandal that today the average life of a commercial building in the UK is just forty years.

We must wake up to this injustice that's being done to us. We must insist on being heard. Too many places are being created by people who are not interested enough in how they make the public feel, and are seeking only to make profit. Money cannot be the value that dominates all others. We must demand that the construction industry places just as much value on the thoughts and feelings of the thousands of women, men and children who have no choice but to experience their buildings every day.

We must demand a world that is less boring.

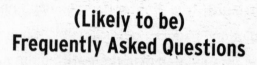

(Likely to be)
Frequently Asked Questions

So you're saying that all new buildings have to look iconic, like the Sydney Opera House?

That would be ridiculous. Of course every new building shouldn't strain to look iconic. I'm only saying that buildings should have enough care, complexity and emotional intelligence built into them that the people who use them and pass them by every day are nourished by them.

Do you just want buildings to look different for difference's sake? Not all of them, but certainly some. Even Haussmann's Parisian streets, which look uniform at first glance, reveal themselves to be full of shifts in visual rhythm when you study them more closely. You might call this 'difference for difference's sake', but I see it as 'interesting for humanity's sake'.

Don't the public only want old-fashioned-looking buildings?

No. The public love new-looking buildings too. They flock to the Eden Project, the Guggenheim, the Sydney Opera House, the Oriental Pearl Tower, and to modern-looking cities like Hong Kong and Tokyo. If the public regularly refer to past architecture styles, it's because they haven't been shown enough good modern alternatives.

You can't measure the worth of a building's appearance by the number of people who like it. Did nobody ever tell you beauty is subjective?

Find me someone who doesn't think Venice is beautiful. Some people prefer tea, some prefer coffee – that's subjective. But almost everyone agrees what constitutes a good cup of coffee. As a planner friend of mine once told me: 'Everyone knows when they're drinking a mug of shit, and that's mostly what we've been drinking since the fifties.'

Isn't this all the fault of property agents and developers?

Agents and developers are definitely complicit in the epidemic of boringness we've become trapped in. But their work is empowered by the Modernist architectural profession, who keep gifting them their drawings for buildings and the language to justify their boringness. This is why I argue that we need a general shift in values for everyone, and that the greatest pressure must come from the public.

Isn't the problem that there aren't enough skilled artisans anymore?

It's important not to be romantic or naive. The days of expensive handcrafted workmanship are gone. But despite our many challenges, society is still richer than at any time in history. We also have the benefit of new ways of forming materials, without lots of expensive craftspeople. 3D printing and the ability to mass-customise using computer technology means that we're no longer in an era where the only economical option is bland, life-denying, repetitive square boxes.

Aren't you ignoring the fact that most buildings aren't designed by architects anyway?

The implication in this question is that there wouldn't have been a disaster of boring if more buildings were designed by architects. I hope by now to have proved this would not be the case.

But it's also true that the anti-complex tastes of the Modernist architects have soaked down through the wider construction industry and given everyone a ready-made excuse to keep making inhuman buildings.

Isn't this all the fault of planners?

They have played a huge part in the problem. But in my experience, planners these days are often desperate to approve more interesting buildings. I think they need to step up and be proud of their humanizing potential, and in turn the construction industry needs to respect them more as representatives of the public.

But surely we can't afford interesting buildings in this unprecedented time of crisis?

Yes, this is a time of extraordinary crisis. But that can't be used as an excuse to keep perpetuating the catastrophe of inhuman buildings. What's actually too expensive is littering the world with more inhuman boxes. We spend trillions on construction every year – and on destruction. This endless destruction is the truly unaffordable option for our health, for society and for the planet.

Are you saying that architects don't care?

Architects certainly do care deeply, otherwise they wouldn't undertake years of training, work long hours and take on a huge amount of responsibility for relatively little pay. The problem is the profession has become desensitised, and doesn't realise it's stopped caring enough about the experience of the ordinary everyday passer-by.

Isn't fussing about the appearance of buildings a right-wing preoccupation? Is the Humanize movement conservative and anti-progressive?

Not at all. Before the Modernist revolution, it was accepted by people of both political sides that public buildings like railway stations, post offices, libraries, schools and swimming pools should be celebratory and generous rather than minimal and mean-spirited. When the authorities built for the people, they did so in a way that showed them respect and dignity and told them they mattered.

I don't believe in a world in which ambition, abundance and generosity are seen as right-wing, whilst submissiveness, boringness and impoverishment are of the left. Neither do I believe in a world in which only the wealthy can afford the daily experience of a nourishing and enjoyable built world. The Humanize movement is truly progressive: it wants everyone, no matter what their background, to be able to live, work, learn, shop and heal in buildings that give back to the individual, the community and the planet.

To the Passer-By

Dear Passer-by,

Have you forgotten that this book is for you?

I hope not. But I've been talking so much about what industry professionals could do to end the catastrophe of boring that by now you'd be forgiven for feeling a little ignored. Even a little powerless.

'What about me?' you might be thinking. 'What can I do about all this? I'm just a person, walking down a street.'

As powerless as you might feel, you're actually the most powerful part of this movement. You're essential to it. Revolutions don't come from council offices or corporate boardrooms or architectural design studios. They come from the street. They start when enough ordinary people come together with enough anger and passion and excitement for change. They happen when everyone begins to make a noise.

This is where the true power lies. With people like you.

And all it takes is four simple acts: looking, feeling, thinking and talking.

When you're out in the streets, look at the buildings that surround you with new eyes. Judge them from the three distances. Ask yourself how they make you feel. Have the confidence to know that your emotional responses truly matter. They are as valid as anyone else's.

Is the building you're looking at interesting enough to hold your attention as you pass it by? If so, why? How have its designers been successful? And if it fails, why?

Encourage your newfound thoughts and feelings to catch fire. When you see brilliance, feel brilliant. When you see boring, feel angry.

Because there's a lot to be angry about. The next time you find yourself surrounded by boring, take a moment to imagine how that place might have looked if the cult had never happened. Visualise how the street would appear if every one of its buildings were interesting enough to hold your attention for the time it took to walk past them. What would the town look like? What would the city look like? If this simple rule were followed, and we hadn't spent the last century collectively suffering a death by a hundred million boring buildings, how much extra joy and fascination would there be in the world?

All of that joy and fascination has been stolen from you. And it's being stolen from you still, by industry professionals who don't care enough about how their work makes ordinary passers-by feel.

Get angry, too, about the ongoing environmental disaster that comes with the endless cycle of putting up unloved buildings, demolishing them, and replacing them with yet more unloved buildings.

But don't let the anger get you down. Let it help you passionately appreciate all the brilliance there is in the buildings, old and new, that do manage to be generous and interesting. Relish these buildings. Celebrate them. Allow them to lift you up and show you the way to a better future in which our streets are lined not with harmful boring but with fascination and joy.

Once you've seen and felt and thought about the buildings that surround you, there is a vital final step. It's critically important that you share your observations and feelings with anyone and everyone who might care. Share your anger. Share your awe. Share your hope. And share this book. Encourage the people you hand it to to then pass it on themselves. Allow its message to spread, slowly but surely, from person to person to person. Allow the revolution to grow and catch alight.

At www.humanise.org you will find resources and suggested reading written by other people who see the problem as I do. You'll also find ways to connect with activists, organisations and creators who are all coming together to fight the war for interesting.

I am going to make a promise to you. I will dedicate the rest of my life to this war. But I need you, dear passer-by, to join us. Our aim is modest: we just want buildings that are not boring! But if we win, we will change the face, and the future, of the planet.

You can be part of the Humanize movement. All you have to do is go out into the street and look, feel, think and talk.

The time has come to open our eyes and make a noise.

The time has come to close the book on boring.

The time has come to Humanize.

THANK YOU

My greatest debt of gratitude goes to Will Storr, my close
collaborator on this book: a brilliant writer, researcher and
friend who took time away from his own important projects
to work with me. For three years, we travelled, thought and
debated together. There could have been no one better to help
crystallise my disconnected thoughts, instincts and ideas
into a coherent, punchy narrative.

Thank you, too, to Gail Rebuck at Penguin Random House
for originally suggesting the idea of a book, and my friend
Mala Gaonkar, who chided me on a regular basis to write
down my ideas and create this manifesto. My agent Elizabeth
Sheinkman has guided me through all stages of the process
and I'm very grateful for her extraordinary support.
At Viking, the patient and good-natured editorial advice
of Daniel Crewe and Greg Clowes has been immensely helpful
and appreciated.

The writings of Jane Jacobs, Jan Gehl and Christopher Alexander
have been hugely influential for me, as for so many others.
I've also been inspired by Richard Rogers, an architect with
the courage and ability to start a national conversation about
the quality of our built environment.

I have drawn on many exciting discussions with a huge
mix of brilliant people, including Dame Sally Davies, Chris
Anderson, Chee Pearlman, Ed Jarvis, Hugo Spiers, Lara
Gregorians and Daniel Glaser. And I want to acknowledge the
wisdom and advice offered so generously by Simon Sinek,
Noreena Hertz, Paul Finch, Paul Morrell and many others.

My clients have taught me how to see projects through
the eyes of the passer-by and our end user. In particular,
Dave Radcliffe, Mary Davidge and Michelle Kaufmann at
Google, and Keith Kerr, with whom I spent many, many
hours discussing the ideas in this book.

Rachel Giles, the studio's publishing manager, has been
incredibly patient, determined and positive, and steered the
book to completion. Ben Prescott, the book's designer, was
wonderfully collaborative and intuitively understood what
I have been trying to express. Cecilia Mackay was relentless
in hunting down exceptional images for the book, and has
been a forensic, creative colleague. Gayle Mault was an
enormous help in the book's early stages.

I also want to thank especially my teenage children, Moss
and Vera, for helping me see buildings through their eyes.
And my partner, Cong, for supporting me with all her
wisdom and love along the way. I'm grateful to my parents,
Hugh Heatherwick and Stefany Tomalin, who nurtured
my fascination with the world and encouraged me to pursue
my passions.

Finally, at Heatherwick Studio, I would like to thank every
team member who has come with me on this extraordinary
thirty-year expedition – with all its ups and downs – exploring
and learning together how to humanize our towns and cities.
With all the trust you've put in me over these years, you've
given me the confidence and experience to write this book.
I can't wait to see what you create next!

SOURCES
PART ONE: HUMAN AND INHUMAN PLACES

Human Places

p. 14, *The straight line*
Megan Cytron, 'Buildings that break the box', *Salon*, 21 February 2011.

p. 16, *After it was completed*
www.lapedrera.com/en/la-pedrera.

p. 19, *When Gaudí was told*
www.lapedrera.com/en/la-pedrera/history.

p. 19, *In the end the pillars*
www.makespain.com/listing/casa-mila-barcelona/.

p. 30, *Gaudí began work*
Alex Greenberger, 'In Barcelona, years-long Sagrada Família completion pushed back by pandemic', *ArtNews*, 17 September 2020.

p. 32, *About 4.5 million people*
'Barcelona's Sagrada Família gets permit after 137 years', *BBC News*, 8 June 2019.

p. 38, *Built in 1975*
https://www.world-architects.com/en/ricardo-bofill-taller-de-arquitectura-barcelona/project/walden-7.

p. 38, *Walden 7 is fourteen storeys*
https://www.archdaily.com/332142/ad-classics-walden-7-ricardo-bofill.

p. 44, *Completed in 1930*
https://www.archiseek.com/2009/1930-marine-building-vancouver-british-columbia/.

p. 44, *fish, seahorses*
Michael Windover, *Art Deco: A Mode of Mobility*, Presses de l'Université du Quebec, 2012, pp. 63–74.

p. 46, *When challenged about*
Ibid., p. 7.

p. 48, *As humans walk through*
Ann Sussman and Justin B. Hollander, *Cognitive Architecture*, Routledge, 2014, p. 17.

The Anatomy of a Catastrophe

p. 100, *It's been estimated*
Charlotte McDonald, 'How many birds are killed by windows?' *BBC News*, 4 May 2013.

p. 112, *A neuroscientist called*
Colin Ellard, *Places of the Heart*, Bellevue Literary Press, 2015, pp. 107–9.

p. 115, *Every single second*
www.britannica.com/science/information-theory/Physiology.

p. 116, *Ellard theorises*
Ellard, p. 112.

p. 117, *One major scientific survey*
J. Sommers and S. J. Vodanovich, 'Boredom proneness: Its relationship to psychological and physical health symptoms', *Journal of Clinical Psychology*, vol. 56, 2000, pp. 149–55.

p. 117, *Reporting by Scientific American*
Anna Gosline, 'Bored to death: Chronically bored people exhibit higher risk-taking behavior', *Scientific American*, 26 February 2007.

p. 117, *Researchers at King's College*
A. Kılıç, W. A. P. van Tilburg and E. R. Igou, 'Risk-taking increases under boredom', *Journal of Behavioral Decision Making*, vol. 33, 2020, pp. 257–69.

p. 117, *Scientists have even found*
W. A. P. van Tilburg and E. R. Igou, 'Going to political extremes in response to boredom', *European Journal of Social Psychology*, vol. 46, 2016, pp. 687–99.

p. 121, *In 2008, scientists*
S. C. Brown et al., 'Built environment and physical functioning in Hispanic elders: The role of "eyes on the street"', *Environmental Health Perspectives*, vol. 116, no. 10, 2008, pp. 1300–1307.

p. 122, *Dr Frances E. Kuo*
Frances E. Kuo, 'Coping with poverty: Impacts of environment and attention in the inner city', *Environment and Behavior*, vol. 33, no. 1, January 2001, pp. 5–34.

p. 123, *Twenty seconds in nature*
Sarah Williams Goldhagen, *Welcome to Your World: How the Built Environment Shapes Our Lives*, HarperCollins, 2017, p. 55.

p. 123, *Incredibly, a simple view*
Ethan Kross, *Chatter: The Voice in Our Head (and How to Harness It)*, Ebury Press, 2021, p. 99.

p. 124, *More recent research*
Chanuki Illushka Seresinhe, Tobias Preis and Helen Susannah Moat 'Using deep learning to quantify the beauty of outdoor places', *Royal Society Open Science*, vol. 4, no. 7, 2017.

p. 124, *One of the researchers*
Chanuki Illushka Seresinhe, 'Natural versus human-built beauty: Which impacts our wellbeing more?' *What Works Wellbeing* [website], 18 October 2019.

p. 125, *A survey of people's*
Maddalena Iovene, Nicholas Boys Smith and Chanuki Illushka Seresinhe, *Of Streets and Squares*, Create Streets, Cadogan, 2019.

p. 129, *A brief chance encounter*
Marwa al-Sabouni, *The Battle for Home: The Vision of a Young Architect in Syria*, Thames and Hudson, 2016, Kindle locations 774, 788, 806.

p. 129, *Then came a new*
Marwa al-Sabouni, 'How Syria's architecture laid the foundation for brutal war', TED Talk, August 2016.

p. 129, *These new neighbourhoods*
al-Sabouni, *The Battle for Home*, 802, 885.

p. 129, *Unlike in the old city*
Ibid., 811, 885.

p. 130, *But al-Sabouni is convinced*
al-Sabouni, TED Talk.

p. 131, *When over 2,000 Americans*
Kriston Capps, 'Classical or modern architecture? For Americans, it's no contest', *Bloomberg*, 14 October 2020.

p. 131, *An analysis of a series*
Ben Southwood, 'Architectural preferences in the UK', *Works in Progress* [newsletter], 29 March 2021.

p. 131, *In 2021, the think tank*
Harry Yorke, 'Public prefers traditional styles to Brutalism in boost for planning reforms', *The Telegraph*, 28 March 2021.

p. 132, *A 2015 survey*
https://corporate.uktv.co.uk/news/article/nations-favourite-buildings-revealed/.

p. 133, *The world's top ten*
James Andrews, 'Every country's favourite architect', *Money* [website], 10 February 2022.

p. 136, *A total of 11 per cent*
World Green Building Council, 'Bringing embodied carbon upfront', https://worldgbc.org/article/bringing-embodied-carbon-upfront/.

p. 136, *It takes 4 kilograms*
'The carbon footprint of a cheeseburger', *SixDegrees* [website], 4 April 2017, https://www.six-degreesnews. org/archives/10261/the-carbon-footprint-of-a-cheeseburger.

p. 136, *It takes 70 kilograms*
'Product Environmental Report, iPhone 12', https://www.apple.com/kr/environment/pdf/products/iphone/iPhone_12_PER_Oct2020.pdf

p. 136, *It takes 4.6 tonnes*
EPA, 'Greenhouse gas emissions from a typical passenger vehicle', www.epa.gov/greenvehicles/greenhouse-gas-emissions-typical-passenger-vehicle.

p. 136, *It takes 16 tonnes*
https://www.nature.org/en-us/get-involved/how-to-help/carbon-footprint-calculator/.

p. 136, *It takes 250 tonnes*
Katharine Gammon, 'How the billionaire space race could be one giant leap for pollution', *The Guardian*, 19 July 2021.

p. 136, *It took 92,210 tonnes*
Reed Landberg and Jeremy Hodges, 'What's wrong with modern buildings? Everything, starting with how they're made', *Bloomberg*, 20 June 2019.

p. 137, *shorter cycles of repair*
Kyle Normandin and Susan Macdonald, *A Colloquium to Advance the Practice of Conserving Modern Heritage*, March 6–7, 2013, Meeting Report, pp. 36, 42–3.

p. 138, *The editor of the*
Will Hurst, 'Demolishing 50,000 buildings a year is a national disgrace', *The Times*, 28 June 2021.

p. 138, *Every twelve months*
'Bringing embodied carbon upfront', https://worldgbc.org/article/bringing-embodied-carbon-upfront/

p. 138, *In the UK, 50,000*
Hurst, 'Demolishing 50,000 buildings'.

p. 138, *the average commercial building*
'Buy Less Stuff', *39 Ways to Save the Planet* [podcast], *BBC Sounds*, 30 August 2021.

p. 139, *In China, 3.2 billion*
EnvGuide, *China Construction and Demolition Waste Disposal Industry Market Report*, June 2021.

p. 143, *plain ignorance*
Stephen Gardiner, *Le Corbusier*, Fontana, 1974, p. 15.

p. 143, *reactionary, conservative*
Joe Mathieson and Tim Verlaan, 'The far right's obsession with modern architecture', failedarchitecture.com, 11 September 2019.

PART TWO: HOW THE CULT OF BORING TOOK OVER THE WORLD

What is an Architect?

p. 161, *In de Architectura*
britannica.com/topic/architecture/Commodity-firmness-and-delight-the-ultimate-synthesis.

p. 166, *The story of what*
The argument that follows is a summary of that which appears in T. J. Heatherwick, 'The Inspiration of Construction: A Case for Practical Making Experience in Architecture', unpublished dissertation, 1991.

p. 169, *By the beginning*
Jackie Craven, 'How did architecture become a licensed profession?', *ThoughtCo.*, 30 January 2020.

p. 182, *Architecture is art*
Lance Hosey, 'Why architecture isn't art (and shouldn't be)', *ArchDaily*, 8 March 2016.

p. 182, *I want to specifically talk*
https://www.paulrudolph.institute/quotes.

p. 182, *Architecture is a visual art*
The Right Angle Journal [online journal], Question no. 4 (Part I).

p. 182, *Architecture is the greatest*
Richard Meier, 'Is Architecture art'? [video], *Big Think*, bigthink.com/videos/is-architecture-art/.

p. 185, *Modernism was an artistic response*
Pericles Lewis, *The Cambridge Introduction to Modernism*, Cambridge University Press, 2007, p. 12.

p. 185, *The art they made*
Ibid., p. 6.

p. 186, *The old rules of painting*
Samuel Jay Keyser, *The Mental Life of Modernism: Why Poetry, Painting, and Music Changed at the Turn of the Twentieth Century*, MIT Press, 2020, p. 1.

p. 186, *The pioneering poet*
Lewis, p. 16.

p. 188, *In the words of Modernist*
Wendy Steiner, *Venus in Exile: The Rejection of Beauty in Twentieth-Century Art*, The Free Press, 2001, p. 61.

p. 188, *the abstract painter*
Barnett Newman, 'The sublime is now', theoria.art-zoo.com/the-sublime-is-now-barnett-newman/.

p. 192, *Ornamentation was seen*
Steiner, p. 79.

p. 192, *Manifesto after manifesto*
Wendy Steiner, 'Beauty is shoe', *Lapham's Quarterly*, https://www.laphamsquarterly.org/arts-letters/beauty-shoe.

Meet the God of Boring

p. 194, *Le Corbusier was surprisingly*
Adam Sharr, *Modern Architecture*, Oxford University Press, 2018, p. 58.

p. 194, *He also saw himself* Le Corbusier, *Towards a New Architecture*, Dover, 1986, p. 110.

p. 196, *Le Corbusier compared*
Ibid., p. 277.

p. 196, *The ancient, winding*
Le Corbusier, *The City of Tomorrow and Its Planning*, Dover, 1987, Kindle location 1128.

p. 198, *Le Corbusier believed*
Corbusier, *Towards a New Architecture*, p. 87.

p. 198, *He liked to tell* Corbusier, *The City of Tomorrow*, 3149.

p. 200, *cost nearly $1,000*
$975 was the publisher's list price on Amazon.com as of June 2021.

p. 200, *other architects sometimes*
Malcolm Millais, *Le Corbusier: The Dishonest Architect*, Cambridge Scholars Publishing, 2017, pp. 30, 52.

p. 203, *suited to simple races*
Corbusier, *Towards a New Architecture*, p. 83.

p. 204, *Decoration is universal*
Gaia Vince, *Transcendence: How Humans Evolved through Fire, Language, Beauty and Time*, Allen Lane, 2019, pp. 129, 132, 134.

p. 204, *Other decorated shells*
Helen Thompson, 'Zigzags on a shell from Java are the oldest human engravings', *Smithsonian Magazine*, 3 December 2014.

p. 205, *Some of the earliest*
Vince, pp. 171, 172.

p. 205, *Earlier still*
https://whc.unesco.org/en/list/1572/.

p. 206, *Even the homes*
Vince, p. 174.

p. 206, *Researchers have found*
Goldhagen, pp. 232, 298.

p. 206, *The bare concrete walls*
Ibid., pp. 55, 57.

p. 209, *He campaigned to have*
Corbusier, *The City of Tomorrow*, 3318, 3274.

p. 210, *He also insisted*
Corbusier, *Towards a New Architecture*,
pp. 31, 153.

p. 212, *In 2021, the team*
Lottie Gross, 'The most beautiful city in
the world – as voted by you', *Rough Guides*
[website], 5 August 2021.

p. 215, *If houses were constructed*
Corbusier, *Towards a New Architecture*, p. 133.

p. 216, *This was demonstrated in 2012*
Pall J. Lindal, Terry Hartig, 'Architectural
variation, building height, and the restorative
quality of urban residential streetscapes',
Journal of Environmental Psychology, vol. 33, 2013,
pp. 26–36.

p. 217, *A century after*
Iovene et al., pp. 6, 76, 174.

p. 219, *We rarely care to look*
Corbusier, *The City of Tomorrow*, 2771.

p. 220, *In 2013, a team*
O. Vartanian et al., 'Preference for curvilinear
contour in interior architectural spaces:
Evidence from experts and nonexperts',
Psychology of Aesthetics, Creativity, and the Arts,
2017.

p. 221, *In another study, participants*
O. Blazhenkova and M. M. Kumar, 'Angular
versus curved shapes: correspondences and
emotional processing', *Perception*, vol. 47,
no. 1, 2018, pp. 67–89.

p. 221, *Elsewhere, researchers*
G. Corradi and E. Munar, 'The Curvature
Effect', in M. Nadal and O. Vartanian (eds),
The Oxford Handbook of Empirical Aesthetics,
Oxford University Press, 2020, pp. 35–52.

p. 221, *Very young children*
Rachel Corbett, 'A new study suggests why
museum architecture is so curvy – and it's
not because visitors like it that way', *ArtNet*,
25 February 2019.

p. 222, *Neuroscientists have found*
Goldhagen, p. 67.

p. 227, *Our streets no longer*
Le Corbusier, *The Radiant City*, Orion Press,
1967, p. 121.

p. 227, *Cafes and places*
Corbusier, *Towards a New Architecture*, p. 61.

p. 228, *Researchers in Seattle*
Tasmin Rutter, 'People are nicer to each other
when they move more slowly': how to create
happier cities', *Guardian*, 8 September 2016.

p. 228, *They also make us*
Goldhagen, p. 110.

p. 230, *Humans are 'thigmotactic'*
Sussman and Hollander, p. 19.

p. 231, *Le Corbusier wanted the Right Bank*
Corbusier, *The City of Tomorrow*, 3274.

p. 231, *Surveys find that*
Iovene et al., p. 6.

p. 233, *To conceive what*
Corbusier, *The City of Tomorrow*, 3289.

p. 235, *Important research by urban*
Alice Coleman, *Utopia on Trial*, Hilary
Shipman, 1985.

p. 235, *According to Robert Gifford*
Nicolas Boys Smith, 'Can high-rise homes
make you ill?', *EG News*, 10 May 2015.

p. 236, *In 1971, filmmakers*
'Where the Houses Used to Be' [documentary],
1971 https://player.bfi.org.uk/free/film/watch-
where-the-houses-used-to-be-1971-online

p. 238, *The Plan proceeds*
Corbusier, *Towards a New Architecture*, p. 177.

p. 240, *In 1929, he built*
Helena Ariza, 'La Cité Frugès: A modern
neighborhood for the working class', architec-
turalvisits.com, 27 January 2015.

p. 240, *The estate agents*
Millais, p. 61.

p. 241, *In 2015 the architecture*
Ariza, 'La Cité Frugès'.

p. 242, *Peter Blake*
Peter Blake, *Le Corbusier*, Penguin, 1960, p. 11.

p. 243, *Charles Jencks*
Charles Jencks, *Le Corbusier and the Tragic View
of Architecture*, Allen Lane, 1973, p. 11.

p. 243, *Stephen Gardiner*
Stephen Gardiner, *Le Corbusier*, Fontana,
1974, p. 14.

p. 247, *The ideas that Le Corbusier*
Sharr, pp. 79–85.

p. 249, *Kenneth Frampton*
Millais, pp. 190, 127.

p. 251, *The slums of the inner cities*
Gus Labin, 'Why architect Le Corbusier want-
ed to demolish downtown Paris',
Business Insider, 20 August 2013.

p. 253, *Mies helped popularise*
'What did Mies van der Rohe mean by less is
more?', phaidon.com/agenda/architecture/
articles/2014/april/02/what-did-mies-van-der-
rohe-mean-by-less-is-more/.

How To (Accidentally) Start a Cult

p. 264, *USE THOSE ELEMENTS*
Corbusier, *Towards a New Architecture*, pp. 16–17.

p. 266, *During much of their*
Patrick Flynn Miriam Dunn, Maureen
O'Connor and Mark Price, *Rethinking the Crit:
A New Pedagogy in Architectural Education*,
ACSA/EAAR Teachers Conference Proceeding,
2019, p. 25.

p. 266, *a rite of passage*
Rachel Sara and Rosie Parnell, 'Fear and
learning in the architectural crit', *Field*, vol. 5,
no. 1, pp. 101–125.

p. 268, *It's long been known*
Joseph Henrich, *The Secret of Our Success*,
Princeton University Press, 2016, pp. 35–53.

p. 268, *In 2017, The Guardian*
Susan Sheahan, 'Advice for student architects:
How to survive the crit', *The Guardian*, 1 Jun 2017.

p. 268, *In an attempt*
Sara and Parnell.

p. 271, *In 2019, a group*
Flynn et al., pp. 25–28.

p. 273, *We have here a figure*
Jacques Derrida, 'The Art of Memoires', trans.
Jonathan Culler, in *Jacques Derrida, Memoires for
Paul De Man*, Columbia University Press, 1986,
pp. 45–88, 72.

p. 275, *This problem has been*
David Halpern, *Mental Health and the Built
Environment*, Taylor & Francis, 1995, pp. 161–3.

p. 280, *What happens to conflict*
tparents.org/Moon-Talks/SunMyungMoon09/
SunMyungMoon-090707.htm.

p. 281, *Heaven's Gate called*
Will Storr, *The Status Game: On Human Life and
How to Play It* , William Collins, 2021, pp. 193–9.

p. 281, *Followers of the Raëlism*
Han Cheung, 'Baptism by DNA transmission',
Taipei Times, 23 August 2017.

p. 283, *archibollocks*
Archibollocks [blog], archibollocks.blogspot.com.

p. 285, *just 6 per cent*
Finn Williams, 'We need architects to work on
ordinary briefs, for ordinary people', *Dezeen*,
4 December 2017.

p. 291, *In 1923, Le Corbusier*
Corbusier, *Towards a New Architecture*, p. 87.

Why Does Everywhere Look Like Profit?

p. 294, *The Industrial Revolution*
Sharr, pp. 4–32.

p. 296, *the arrival of the railways*
Ibid., p. 24.

p. 300, *Over a million houses*
https://www.britannica.com/event/the-Blitz.

p. 300, *19 per cent in Japan*
Tatiana Knoroz, 'The Rise and Fall of Danchi',
ArchDaily, 19 February 2020.

p. 303, *According to the architect*
Von Romain Leick et al., 'A new look at
Germany's postwar reconstruction', *Der Spiegel*,
10 August 2010.

p. 306, *The iconic Scottish*
'Billy Connolly: Made in Scotland', bbc.co.uk/
programmes/b0bwzhy6.

p. 310, *In 1967, 45 per cent*
Jean Twenge, *Generation Me*, Atria, 2006, p. 99.

p. 310, *A 2015 survey*
Shelly Schwarz, 'Most Americans, rich or
not, stressed about money: Surveys', *CNBC*,
3 August 2015.

p. 310, *A major global survey*
IPSOS, *Global Attitudes on Materialism, Finances
and Family; The Global Trends Survey: A Public
Opinion Report Key Challenges Facing the World*,
13 December 2013.

p. 312, *According to the urban*
Samuel Stein, *Capital City*, Verso, 2019, p. 2.

p. 312, *He told me that*
Conversation between Thomas Heatherwick
and Paul Morrell, 11 March 2022.

p. 324, *Building designers are*
Oliver Wainwright, 'Are building regulations
the enemy of architecture?', *The Guardian*,
28 February 2013.

p. 324, *The architects Liam Ross*
L. Ross and T. Onabolu, *Venice Take Away: The
British Pavilion at the 13th Venice Architecture
Biennale/RIBA Ideas to Change British Architecture
Season: British Standard Lagos Exception*,
AA Publications, 2012.

p. 336, *A politician's first thought*
Conversation between Thomas Heatherwick
and Paul Morrell, 11 March 2022.

PART THREE: HOW TO RE-HUMANIZE THE WORLD

Changing How We Think

p. 363, *Back in the 1960s*
https://www.nas.gov.sg/archivesonline/
blastfromthepast/gardencity.

p. 379, *I learned about*
Loukas Karnis, 'How Steve Jobs became the Gutenberg of our times', typeroom [website], 15 July 2016.

p. 379, *A high-security*
Yoni Heisler, 'Inside Apple's secret packaging room', *Network World*, 24 January 2012.

p. 379, *Packaging can be*
Karen Blumenthal, *Steve Jobs: The Man Who Thought Different*, Bloomsbury, 2012, p. 208.

Elephants in the Room

p. 426, *We smoke less*
Xiochen Dai et al., 'Evolution of the global smoking epidemic', *Tobacco Control*, vol. 31, 2022, pp. 129–37.

p. 426, *use seatbelts more*
'Stronger "buckle up" laws change attitudes among young drivers', *UCL News*, 21 October 2022.

p. 426, *a greater number*
https://www.statista.com/topics/8771/
veganism-and-vegetarian-ism-worldwide/.

p. 426, *Following outrage*
Calla Wahlquist, 'It took one massacre: How Australia embraced gun control after Port Arthur', *The Guardian*, 14 March 2016.

p. 426, *In 2005 we banned*
Jo Revill and Amelia Hill, 'Victory for Jamie in school meal war', *The Observer*, 6 March 2005.

p. 428, *The pre-World War*
Michael Benedikt, '18 ways to make architecture matter', *Common Edge*, 8 February 2022.

p. 429, *But the simultaneous*
Anu Madgavkar, Jonathan Woetzel and Jan Mischke, 'Global wealth has exploded. Are we using it wisely?', *McKinsey Global Institute* [website], 26 November 2021.

p. 429, *The amount we threw*
'Global construction trends', *Market Prospects* [website], 13 August 2021.

p. 432, *The global waste* 'The global construction and demolition waste market is estimated to be USD 26.6 billion in 2021', *Yahoo! Finance*, 13 October 2021.

p. 432, *In the US, around 90*
'28 incredible statistics about waste generation', *Stone Cycling* [website], 3 September 2021.

Changing What We Do

p. 438, *The architect suffers*
Norman Shaw and T. G. Jackson (eds), *Architecture: A Profession or an Art, Thirteen Short Essays on the Qualifications and Training of Architects*, John Murray, 1892, p. xxviii.

p. 438, *What we are protesting*
Ibid., p. 69.

p. 439, *the image of self-made*
Sharr, p. 24.

p. 451, *Block by Block*
https://www.blockbyblock.org/projects/beirut

p. 467, *The designer*
Alyn Griffiths, 'Joshua Vermillion: How AI Art Tools Could Revolutionize Architectural Design', *WEPRESENT* [website] 9 May 2023.

p. 471, *By 2050, two out*
Goldhagen, p. xviii.

PICTURE CREDITS

All images are copyright Heatherwick Studio, unless stated below. Every effort has been made to contact all copyright holders. We will be pleased to amend in future editions any errors or omissions brought to our attention.

Numbers refer to page numbers. Additional photography credits are given in brackets.

Abbreviations:
t = top   l = left
c = centre   r = right
b = bottom

123rf.com: 209 (*wrecking ball*)
4CornersImages: 18, 150–151 (Luigi Vaccarella); 155 b (Sebastian Wasek); 158 bl, 404–5 (Maurizio Rellini); 223 (Ben Pipe); 388 l (Aldo Pavan); 391 bl (Massimo Borchi)
ACME: 357 t & b (Jack Hobhouse)
Adobestock: 406
akg-images: 191 bl (Interfoto/Sammlung Rauch), 195 (Keystone), 244–6 (Schütze/Rodemann), 255 tl (Mondadori Portfolio/Archivio Fabrizio Carraro), 302, 305
Alamy: 16 l & r, 27 c, 47 bc, 47 bl, 47 tr, 60–61, 64–5, 77 t, 80 b, 81 t, 104, 108 c, 126 t, 127 t, 140, 156 b, 162, 165 l, 166 t & b, 188–9, 203 tl, 207, 213 b, 219 t, 219 b, 229, 234, 313, 314–5, 352, 355 t, 390 tr, 397 r, 399 t, 403, 407, 408–9, 436–7, 455, 468
Alessi: 378
Alexander Turnbull Library, Wellington: 155t (Albert Percy Godber)
AntiStatics Architecture: 390 bl (Xia Zhi)
Archmospheres: 108b (Marc Goodwin)
Ashley Sutton Design: 334 b
AVR London: 26 l (Matthew White)
© **Iwan Baan:** 385, 418–19
© **Murray Ballard:** 353 br
Peter Barber: 366–7
© **Bed Images:** 360–61
Ben Harrison Photography: 353 tr
Ben Prescott Design: 26–7 (*crack*), 54–5, 96–7, 286, 311, 318, 319, 391 br, 399 b, 415, 446, 474–85
Bigstock: 101, 156 tr; 316
Block by Block (www.blockbyblock.org): 451 l
Karl Blossfeldt: 224–5

Bridgeman Images: 13, 126 b & 127 b (Christie's); 186 & 187 (Private Collection); 190 tl (Maidstone Museum & Art Gallery); 190 tr (Kunstmuseum, Basel); 398 (Look & Learn)
© **Camera Press London:** 102 (Michael Wolf/© Estate of Michael Wolf/LAIF)
© **Brett Cole:** 118–19
Columbia University Rare Book & Manuscript Library: 197 t
Design Council Archive, University of Brighton Design Archives: 171
Jinnifer Douglass (www.jinyc-photo.com): 113
Dreamstime: 29, 32, 98–9, 109 t
Flickr Creative Commons: 47 tl & tc (Sandra Cohen-Rose and Colin Rose); 47 br (Louise Jayne Munton); 387 (CharlieRomeo123)
Fondation Le Corbusier: 239, 240
Foster + Partners: 108 t (Chris Goldstraw), 389 (Nigel Young)
Getty Images: 28 t, 28 tc, 28 tr, 34 b, 68–9, 110–11, 120, 124–5, 134–5, 138–9 b, 142, 152, 158 br, 158 t, 159 b, 163, 197 b, 198–9, 201, 203 tl & br, 215, 227, 230, 233, 236, 242, 243, 250–51, 253, 254 bl & br, 255 tr, bl & br, 258–9, 260–61, 272, 280, 298–9, 301, 307, 333, 396 l & r, 449
Heatherwick Archives: 173 t, 175 l, 179 bl, 179 br, 180, 181 b & r
Heatherwick Studio: 9, 10–11, 27 r, 56–83, 209 (*wrecking ball model*), 328–9, 348–9, 381, 391 tl, 425 t, 462 (Raquel Diniz); 165 r, 357 c & b, 388 r (Rachel Giles); 28 c & l, 42–3, 49–50, 72, 73, 78, 84, 132–3, 355 b & c, 359 b & c, 362, 368, 371, 387, 390 br (Thomas Heatherwick); 461, 463 (Pintian Liu); 442–3 (Jethro Rebollar); 90, 204–5, 266, 268–9, 276–7 (Olga Rienda); 460 (Joanna Sabak); 422–3
© **Clemens Gritl:** 210–211
Groupwork: 359 t (Tim Soar)
© **Historic England Archive:** 237 (John Laing Photographic Collection)
Historic Environment Scotland: 306 (© Crown Copyright)
Houghton Library, Harvard University: 168
Hufton + Crow: 26 r, 420, 421

Selected architectural works featured
in the text:

26–7 The world as it might be
The Arches, Highgate, London. The DHaus
Company, 2023: 26 l

The Glasshouse, Woolbeding. Heatherwick
Studio, 2022: 26 r

L'Arbre Blanc, Montpellier. Sou Fujimoto,
Nicolas Laisné, Manal Rachdi et Dimitri
Roussel, 2019: 27 c

Little Island, New York City. Heatherwick
Studio, 2021: 27 r

108–9 When is Boring Not Boring?
House of Wisdom, Sharjah. Foster + Partners,
2020: 108 t

Jatiya Sangsad Bhaban, Dhaka. Louis Khan,
1982: 108 cr

Fyyri Library, Kirkkonummi. JKMM
Architects, 2020: 108 b

Len Lye Centre, Govett-Brewster Art Museum,
New Plymouth. Patterson Associates, 2015:
109 t

Royal Crescent, Bath. John Wood the Younger,
1774: 109 cl

Protiro Rehabilitation Centre, Caltigirone.
NOWA, 2016: 109 cr

Cimitero Monumentale di San Cataldo, Rome.
Aldo Rossi and Gianni Braghieri, 1971: 109 b

289 Postmodernism and Brutalism
AT&T Building (550 Madison Avenue),
New York. Philip Johnson and John Burgee,
1984: 289 l

Buffalo City Court Building, Buffalo. Pfohl,
Roberts and Biggie, 1974: 289 r

352–3 City, Street, Door
Kring GumHo Culture Centre, Seoul.
Unsangdong Architects, 2008: 352 t, c, b

Liberty, London. Edwin Thomas and Edwin
Stanley Hall, 1924: 353 tl, cl, bl

The Diamond, University of Sheffield.
Twelve Architects, 2015: 353 tr, cr, br

388–90 Prioritise Door Distance
Bund Finance Center. Shanghai. Designed
jointly by Foster + Partners Heatherwick
Studio, 2017: 389 t

MaoHaus, Beijing. AntiStatics Architecture,
2017: 390 bl

408–9 Necessary Visual Complexity
Centre Pompidou, Paris. Renzo Piano, Richard
Rogers and Gianfranco Franchini, 1977

Images drawn from other publications:

Philippe Boudon, *Lived-In Architecture: Le
Corbusier's Pessac Revisited*, The MIT Press,
Cambridge, 1979. Original edition © 1969
Dunod, Paris: 241

Lewis Nockalls Cottingham, *The Smith and
Founder's Director*, 1824: 414 t

John Crunden, *The Joiner and Cabinet Maker's
Darling*, 1770: 413 l

Theodor Däubler and Iwan Goll, *Archipenko-Album*, pub. G. Kiepenheuer, 1921: 190 tr

William Halfpenny, *Practical Architecture*, 1724: 413–14 b & c

Batty Langley, *Gothic Architecture Improved by Rules and Proportions*, 1747: 411, 413–4 b & c

Neknisk Ukeblad, 1893: 148

Giorgio Vasari, *Le vite de' piv eccellenti pittori, scvltori, e architettori*, 1568: 168

Vitruvius, *De architectura libri decem*, 1649: 160

Rainer Zerbst, *Gaudi*, Benedikt Taschen Verlag, 1988: 9–11

William H. Whyte, *The Social Life of Small Urban Spaces*, Project for Public Spaces, 1980: 231

Woman's Own, December 1981: 170 a

With special thanks to:
Big Sky Studios, Kacper Chmielewski, DawkinsColour, Irem Dökmeci, Mason Francis Wellings-Longmore, Grace Giles, Simon Goodwin, Fred Manson, Stepan Martinowsky, Dirce Medina Patatuchi, Diana Mykhaylychenko, Leah Nichols, Peter Pawsey, Bethany Rolston, Julian Saul, Emric Sawyer, Ray Torbellin, Annie Underwood, Cong Wang, Pablo Zamorano.

Copyeditor: Gemma Wain
Proofreaders: Bethany Holmes and Nancy Marten

JOIN THE
HUMANIZE
MOVEMENT

Sign up at <u>humanise.org</u> if you want to make our cities more joyful and human.

THE WEBSITE IS FILLED WITH IDEAS AND RESOURCES:

- The latest research in the battle against boring – from the fields of architecture, neuroscience, social science, psychology and more

- Resources – suggested reading and links to campaigning organisations

- Practical ways for all of us to help tackle this problem that silently affects billions of people's lives.

Follow us on Instagram **@humaniseorg** and other social media channels to express your ideas, outrage, curiosity, and amazement at the buildings that surround us.

HAVE AN OPINION. START A CONVERSATION.
DEMAND BETTER.